THE GOOD LIFE

JEFFREY B. RUBIN

THE GOOD LIFE

psychoanalytic reflections on

love, ethics, creativity, and spirituality

STATE UNIVERSITY OF NEW YORK PRESS

Published by
STATE UNIVERSITY OF NEW YORK PRESS
ALBANY

© 2004 State University of New York

For information, address State University of New York Press,
90 State Street, Suite 700, Albany, NY 12207

Production, Laurie Searl
Marketing, Anne M. Valentine

Library of Congress Cataloging in Publication Data

Rubin, Jeffrey B.
  The good life : psychoanalytic reflections on love, ethics,
creativity, and spirituality / Jeffrey B. Rubin.
      p. cm.
  Includes bibliographical references and index.
  ISBN 0-7914-6215-3 (alk. paper) — ISBN 0-7914-6216-1 (pbk. : alk. paper)
  1. Psychoanalysis. 2. Conduct of life. I. Title.
BF175.R82 2004
150.19'5—dc22

                                        2004008927

10 9 8 7 6 5 4 3 2 1

This book is dedicated to four teachers, whose wisdom, guidance, and support have immeasurably aided my efforts to understand myself and live a good life.

George Atwood

David Kastan

Joel Kramer

Monte Ullman

And to John Moody, best friend every step of the way.

Contents

PREFACE

<hr>

> Since psychoanalysis is my home, I feel free not to treat it
> politely. It needs constant upkeep and can always use renewal.
> —Robert Stoller

PSYCHOANALYSIS HAS BEEN an endless source of enlightenment and inspiration to me for the past twenty-four years. Encountering it in my twenties was undoubtedly one of the most auspicious and formative experiences of my life. Psychoanalysis has transformed my life by opening up vast and subtle vistas on human motivation and relationships that I doubt I would ever have discovered in any other way.

Psychoanalysis is increasingly marginalized in our postmodern world, where everything is deconstructed and debunked from reason to revelation, and standards of ethics are leveled and homogenized. Egocentricity, hedonism, popular psychospiritual quick fixes, and self-anesthetizing and addictive behavior serve for too many people in Western culture as misguided substitutes for the good life. These bleached-out versions of a life well-lived leave us spiritually hungry and cast adrift without any guiding direction for action, and desperate for solutions to address the malaise and alienation that plague us.

I find it ironic that psychoanalysis is increasingly attacked, if not dismissed, at the very moment when it has a seminal and profound contribution to make to contemporary reflections on what afflicts us, and what might heal and sustain us. Articulating these contributions is crucial to the renewal of psychoanalysis in the twenty-first century.

A central theme of one of my earlier books, *A Psychoanalysis for Our Time: Exploring the Blindness of the Seeing I,* was that for psychoanalysis to actualize its emancipatory potential and illuminate how we could live with greater depth and intimacy, joy and meaning, it must draw on its hidden resources as well as confront its blind spots and omissions. To do this, I recommended that psychoanalysts examine topics that had been sorely neglected in the field, such as the psychology of love and creativity, the moral dimensions of the analytic process, and the role of spirituality on identity.[1]

The Good Life picks up where my previous book ended by exploring, from a new perspective, marginalized topics essential to the revitalization of psychoanalysis and society. Psychoanalysis at its best elucidates both the ingredients of love, ethics, creativity, spirituality, and the life well-lived *and* the obstacles to experiencing them. Exploring the good life from this dual perspective provides an indispensable resource for helping us live with greater meaning and vitality in the twenty-first century.

"There is another world and it is in this one," the French surrealist poet Paul Eluard reminds us. I hope that grappling with the nature of love, ethics, creativity, spirituality, and the good life will disclose something of the aliveness and ecstasy of this other world within our own that makes life worth living.

ACKNOWLEDGMENTS

NO WRITER EVER WORKS ALONE. I am deeply grateful for the invaluable support and assistance provided by friends and colleagues ranging from reading individual chapters to steering me toward interesting lines of research. This book was deeply enriched by conversations with Diana Alstad, Neil Altman, Emma Anderson, Lew Aron, George Atwood, Claude Barbre, Jim Barron, Lori Bohm, Mark Branitsky, Jean Bratman, Lou Breger, Peter Carnochan, Robin Cohen, Susan Cohen, Paul Cooper, Rebecca Curtis, Doris Dlugacz, Marianne Horney Eckardt, Mike Eigen, Mark Finn, Jerry Garguilo, Jerry Gold, Karen Faccenda Healy, James Jones, Don Kalshed, David Kastan, Joel Kramer, Amaury Larancuent, E. Betty Levin, Dorthy Levinson, JoAnn Magdoff, Barry Magid, Esther Menaker, Louise Reiner, Alan Roland, George Silbershatz, Randy Sorenson, Mary Traina, Ann Ulanov, Barry Ulanov, Brent Willock, Avi Winokur, and Victoria Wyndham. I am also grateful to the two anonymous reviewers from the State University of New York Press, whose feedback enriched the manuscript, and to Rosemary Wellner for her skillful copyediting.

Steven O'Neill, Michelle McKee, and David Ward of the Kristine Mann Library of the Analytical Psychology Club of New York provided able bibliographic assistance—as did Matthew Vonunwerth from the library of the New York Psychoanalytic Institute.

An earlier version of chapter one, "Psychoanalysis and Creative Living" was published in *The Journal of the American Academy of Psychoanalysis and Dynamic Psychiatry* (32, 2: 361–380). A section of an earlier version of chapter two, "Values and Ethics in Psychoanalysis" was published in *Where Id Was: Normalization in Psychoanalysis* (Continuum, 2001) edited by Anthony Molino. I presented an earlier version of chapter four, "There's More Than Meets the I: Psychoanalytic Reflections on Spirituality" at the August 2000 meeting of Division 36 of the American Psychological Association in Washington, DC. A section of an earlier version of chapter five, "Psychoanalysis and the Good Life" appeared in *Psychoanalysis and Buddhism: An Unfolding Dialogue* (Wisdom Publications, 2003) edited by Jeremy Safran. I am grateful to Ulla Schnell of

Continuum Press and Rod Meade-Sperry of Wisdom Publications for their speedy assistance in granting me permission to reprint my work.

A special thanks to Hilary de Bhál Sweeney for her beautiful and evocative cover art and design.

I would like to thank Jane Bunker, Senior Acquisitions Editor, Laurie Searl, Senior Production Editor, and Anne Valentine, Senior Marketing Manager of the State University of New York Press for their skillful expediting of the publication process. They were a joy to work with.

INTRODUCTION

This craft of ours, sacred and bright,
The world is lit by it without light.
—Anna Akhmatova

There are two things I wanted to do:
I wanted to show the things that had to be
corrected; I wanted to show the things that had
to be appreciated.
—Lewis W. Hine

WALKING THROUGH THE National Gallery of Art in Washington, DC, several years ago, I was immediately drawn to the canvasses of Thomas Cole, a key figure in the Hudson River school, America's first native school of landscape painting (1825–1875). His lush, richly colored depictions of pastoral river valleys, spiritually luminous and enlivening clouds, skies, and light, and vast reaches of mountains and forests were quite different in style, content, and emotional resonance from the Impressionistic and Abstract Expressionist artists (such as Monet, Renoir, Kandinsky, Gaston, and Diebenkorn) who usually stimulate and inspire me. Cole's canvasses convey Edenic purity, the terrors of civilization, intimations of new beginnings and fresh starts, and the dangers of "progress." They evoked in me feelings of wonder and beauty, dread and sacredness. As I reflected on my interest in these paintings I realized that they resonated with my experiences as a psychoanalyst, where I am privy on a daily basis (sometimes even within the same session!) to a vast range of feelings and experiences including love and alienation, spirituality and immorality, creativity and perversion. I was moved most of all by the harmonious coexistence in Cole's paintings of a variety of moods and themes that are often separated and dichotomized such as beauty and foreboding, mutability and eternity, exploitation and spirituality, and critique and affirmation.

1

While we psychoanalysts are experts in hatred, envy, and perversions, we seem like neophytes in love, ethics, creativity, spirituality, and the good life. We all too often focus on what afflicts and depletes people, and neglect what nurtures and vitalizes them. Psychoanalysis has often slighted the life-enriching possibilities of love, spirituality, and creativity in its attempt to elucidate the psychopathology of these experiences. To speak of narcissism, aggression, and depression without speaking of love, ethics, creative living, and the good life—as the vast majority of analysts do—could contribute to the very human suffering that psychoanalysis is designed to address.

When I was younger, I use to think that the focus in psychoanalysis on what ails us—from afflictive emotions (jealousy, hate, and sadism) to troubled relationships—was somehow a testament to psychoanalysis's depth. Equating depth with an appetite for the grim side of life, I assumed, perhaps like many psychoanalysts, that psychoanalysis was shunning the false salvations and illusory Band-Aids offered by those more faint of heart such as popular psychospiritual writers and contemplative and religious seekers. In its attention to the dreary underside of life, I too readily assumed that psychoanalysis was getting at the real truth of people and the world.

"[T]he highest goods of humanity," writes Freud, are "research, art, love, ethical and social sense."[1] "It is not our intention," Freud had earlier asserted, "to dispute the noblest endeavours of human nature."[2] Although these may be the noblest human pursuits, ironically, it is difficult to find many systematic or illuminating treatments of them in the psychoanalytic literature that appreciate their complexity without reducing their value. I find it odd—and worthy of further psychoanalytic scrutiny—that psychoanalysis neglects those topics that give life meaning and make people feel most alive.

Attacked in the media, maligned by its critics, psychoanalysis as a discipline is suffering—losing cultural prestige and appeal. And yet, at the very moment when psychoanalysis is under increasing public attack and confronts declining enrollments in its institutions, it evinces internal vitality, undergoing a great deal of meaningful transformation. The relational revolution of the past decade and a half, with its appreciation of the analyst's conscious and unconscious participation in the treatment, and the dyadic nature of human development and the treatment process (by which I mean the fact that infants are raised and develop in particular interpersonal environments and patients attempt to understand themselves and change in specific therapeutic contexts) has challenged and transformed many traditional and received analytic theories and practices. Many contemporary psychoanalysts, for example, now view the contribution of analysand and analyst to the treatment process in a more fertile and nuanced light. Analysts from many different theoretical perspectives have illuminated with greater precision subtle faces of the analytic relationship and interaction and the analysts's experience, including how to constructively use the analysts's subjective interior life and the interpersonal patterns and enactments in the therapeutic relationship as a potential resource in understanding disavowed dimensions of the patient's experience. Contemporary psychoanalysts have opened up new vistas in understanding human development and the therapeutic relationship and in alleviating human suffering.

In the face of vitriolic attacks on its theories and practices, psychoanalysts are ironically unanalytic—looking outward rather than inward—in confronting our disciplinary difficulties. We blame our disciplinary crisis on external circumstances: the antianalytic public climate, the popularity of quick-fix palliatives, managed care, and the declining pool of potential analysands because of the economic downturn that all but the very wealthy are experiencing.

But I wonder if we contribute—perhaps inadvertently—to our own marginalization and disempowerment. Are some of our problems as a discipline of our own making? Is our declining public respect due, at least in part, to our failure to address topics of vital importance to most people?

Psychoanalysis is suffering, in my view, because of its unworldliness; its detachment from the universe in which it is practiced; and because it has abandoned meaning-making and moral reflectiveness to other disciplines. The provincialism of psychoanalysis has been detrimental to its own standing in the larger universe of discourse that it shapes.

It is tempting in the face of proliferating attacks on our discipline and our professional identities to become more defensive and insular by carving out smaller and smaller areas in which we can be experts. Reading the contemporary postclassical relational literature is sometimes an experience of postmodern subjectivity and self-preoccupation, as analysts focus on ever smaller units of analysis such as their own internal processes and their impact on the treatment. The result of this introverted focus has been damaging as well as salutary.

I think we need to proceed in the opposite direction. Speaking to fellow poets, but in language apropos to psychoanalysts, Stanley Kunitz counsels: "[I]t would be healthier if we could locate ourselves in the thick of life, at every intersection where values and meanings cross, caught in the dangerous traffic of self and universe."[3]

Psychoanalysis will benefit greatly from becoming more cosmopolitan—moving out of its hermeticism and narcissism into the larger social world it, like the analytic dyad, partakes in—as well as refining its understanding of the nature of the analyst's unconscious experience and his or her hidden influence on the therapeutic relationship. Psychoanalysis needs to widen its scope to include issues that it has previously neglected, including love, morality, spirituality and creativity.[4]

It is especially crucial that we psychoanalysts address these topics because of the demoralized and alienating times we live in. Our world is increasingly troubled and adrift. Cynicism and pessimism reign. Increasing numbers of people are depleted by cognitive oversaturation and the multiple and conflicting demands placed on them. There is insufficient time for self-reflection and introspection. Many domains of our lives from politics to professional sports resemble a moral free-for-all characterized by rampant egocentricity and a disregard for others. Aesthetic and moral standards are leveled as marketability, easy digestability, and sensationalism masquerade as quality and depth. As contemporary novels, movies, and television programs focus much more on betrayal, infidelity, egocenticity, and immorality than creativity, love, or ethics, people increasingly hunger for ideals to believe in. Hedonism, conspicuous consumption, quick-fix pop psychospiritual solutions, and self-anesthetizing behavior serve as substitutes.

There are two sources of interpretive error, according to Freud: "the Scylla of underestimating the importance of the repressed unconscious, and the Charybdis of judging the normal entirely by the standards of the pathological."[5] Because secular and spiritual conceptions of love, ethics, creativity, spirituality, and the good life generally partake of the first source of interpretive error— "underestimating the importance of the repressed unconscious"—they serve as an inadequate foundation for elucidating these topics. Secular thought— embodied in contemporary popular self-help writings—usually offers degraded visions of these issues, while spiritual traditions present quixotic ones. Many people feel emotionally alienated and deprived and morally at sea because they lack answers to essential questions about how to live; nor do they have a clear direction for obtaining those answers.

It is fashionable in our time to claim that psychoanalysis is a relic of a bygone age. I think psychoanalysis is actually more crucial and vital to our collective mental health than ever before. This suggests a discipline that is more complicated and less dismal than critics acknowledge. Psychoanalysis has a great deal to contribute to the emotional bankruptcy that confronts us. It has the potential to illuminate where we have gone awry and how we might live in more harmonious and vital ways.

Psychoanalysis offers a sanctuary from the cognitive oversaturation and pressure to live flattened lives that permeate our culture.[6] Ordinary life collapses and impoverishes (if not shatters) psychic space and human subjectivity. The analytic environment is potentially a sacred, liminal space, devoid of the manifold impingements (cell phones, pagers, e-mails, and faxes) that can foster self-alienation as they compromise our intimacy with ourselves. Psychoanalysis is a "hermeneutics of suspicion"—challenging and attempting to demystify taken-for-granted motives and meanings.[7] In its attention to unconscious dimensions of human selfhood, psychoanalysis has access to depths of human subjectivity that are not explored anywhere else in daily life, including religious and spiritual disciplines.

Psychoanalysis has the potential—which it does not always actualize—of approaching human experience from a unique vantage point, one that simultaneously illuminates what inhibits us and what might nourish and sustain us. Eluding the pessimistic implications of those strands of postmodern thought that lead to amoral aestheticism and nihilism[8] and the buoyant and illusory optimism that characterizes much contemplative thought and the self-help industry, a visionary psychoanalysis could appreciate the beauty in ourselves and the world while looking unflinchingly at what is wrong and needs transformation. Such a liberatory psychoanalysis—like some of the Hudson River canvasses of Thomas Cole—has the potential for a more nuanced and balanced perspective on creative living, love, ethics, spirituality, and the good life. It can confront immorality yet foster ethics. It can address the obstacles to intimacy while simultaneously illuminating what facilitates a loving relationship.

Illuminating the well-lived life demands a creative rather than masterful or perverse approach toward it. McDougall and Bach[9] distinguish between creativity and perversion. In perverse scenarios an author/director sets up a rigid, preprogrammed script that is unilaterally imposed on a passive, disenfranchised other who is treated as a means to the author's ends. The subjugated person has no power and is exploited by the author of the perverse scenario. Creativity, on the other hand, is a way of living, making, and relating to self and others that is fresh, vital, unpredictable, and open to feedback and evolution. Psychoanalysis is ambivalent about creativity and its own creative potential. On the one hand, psychoanalysis offers enormous resources for elucidating obstacles to creativity. On the other hand, when we analysts know too much beforehand about what a work of art really means or the fundamental and singular motives of creativity, then psychoanalysis unconsciously partakes of a perverse scenario in which the work of art serves as merely a means to the author's ends and is psychologically colonized. When psychoanalysis is The-Discipline-That-Knows, then art has nothing new to teach psychoanalysts and our discipline is impoverished.

The first chapter, "Psychoanalysis and Creative Living," examines the tension within psychoanalysis between its creativity and its perversity. Working through this problem is essential to liberate psychoanalysis from the shackles of its self-blindness so that it can experience its emancipatory potential. Then psychoanalysis can foster creative living as well as provide a richer perspective to examine love, morality, spirituality, and the good life.

Many analysts since Freud's day have embraced the ideal of the analyst as a neutral scientist dispensing objective information to the patient. Values and ethics are eclipsed when scientific objectivity and neutrality are one's ideals. And yet, despite the conscious ideal of moral neutrality, analysts have a variety of unconscious conceptions of ethics and how the patient will learn how to live morally, which deeply shape the analytic experience. "Values and Ethics in Psychoanalysis," chapter two, delineates the three extant stances that have dominated the way analysts have dealt with these issues: the phobic attitude of those analysts wedded to the ideal of neutrality toward values and the Platonic role of analysts who believe that helping the patient get in touch with Reality (or since Jung and Winnicott, "the Self") will give them direction for how to live. Since "reality" and self-experience are complex and multi-dimensional rather than straightforward and singular, none of these approaches is sufficient for helping patients navigate the complex and ever-shifting waters of our postmodern world.

With its attention to the relational matrix in human development and psychoanalytic treatment, postclassical relational analysis seems to provide a way out of the cul-de-sac that psychoanalytic reflections on values and ethics have led to. Contemporary relational thought represents a vast improvement over the Platonic and scientistic conceptions of the analyst. But the potential of relational thought is compromised by a hidden egocentricity underlying its conception of self that emerges when patients bring interpersonal moral dilemmas to treatment. In this chapter, I argue that new possibilities for patients emerge when the analyst is an Aristotelian aiding the patient in cultivating "phronesis" or moral know-how rather than a Platonist helping the patient get in touch with the Real or the Self.

"We must begin to love in order not to fall ill," claims Freud, "and we are bound to fall ill if we are unable to love."[10] Despite the fact that love is essential to our mental and physical health, its fate in our world is troubling. Movies and television decry the possibility of love, depicting betrayal and infidelity, rather than loving commitments. Contemporary psychospiritual traditions present an idealized and illusory version of love that is belied by the pervasive experience of failed unions. In chapter three, "Psychoanalysis at Play in the Garden of Love," I examine the ambivalent relationship that psychoanalysis has about love. On the one hand, love has been relatively neglected in psychoanalytic discourse. Psychoanalysis has focused more on "falling in love" than what sustains it. On the other hand, psychoanalysis has the potential to elucidate the psychological dimensions of a loving relationship. Drawing on Winnicott's notion of potential space and Wilkinson and Gabbard's[11] notion of romantic space, this chapter explores those factors that contribute to and sustain a loving relationship. Such a relationship is characterized by openness, playfulness, mutual validation, an acceptance of differences and multiple perspectives on reality and the relationship, and a harmonious integration of apparent opposites (such as passion and reflectiveness, individuation and merger, and security and risk).

There is a burgeoning interest in spirituality in our world and in psychoanalysis. Within the last few years, a spate of anthologies, books, and conferences have explored the possible intersection between psychoanalysis and the spiritual quest. Spirituality is of increasing interest to psychoanalysts and patients in treatment. In chapter four, "There's More than Meets the I: Psychoanalytic Reflections on Spirituality," I explore what authentic spirituality is, why there is so much interest in it at this cultural moment, how spiritual experiences can enrich psychoanalysis and self-experience, and how psychoanalytic understandings might help spiritual seekers avoid a variety of potential pathologies of spirit. After demonstrating that spirituality is an experience of a self-transcending (and often self-enlivening and expanding) relationship between self and the universe beyond ourselves, rather than a possession or a developmental achievement, I delineate a variety of pathologies of spirituality and the spiritual quest. I point toward a contemplative psychoanalysis that explores both the enriching and pathological facets of spiritual experiences.

People can psychologically and spiritually "die" before their physical deaths, as Tolstoy's Ivan Ilyich reminds us, from a life that is not really lived. The commitment to respecting and not infringing on the patient's autonomy and freedom traditionally makes Socratic questions about how one might live the good life seem outside the bounds of psychoanalysis. But to know what a cure is, to know when to terminate treatment, a psychoanalyst must have conscious and unconscious images of a good life. Two conceptions dominate contemporary speculations about this topic: a materialistic, secular one and a romanticized and selfless spiritual one. Both are problematic. Psychoanalysis has something important to contribute to this topic. Chapter five, "Psychoanalysis and the Good Life" examines the implicit and explicit conceptions of the well-lived life in various schools of analysis, including classical, object relational, self-psychological, and interpersonal analysis. It also addresses implications for freedom and conceptions of self.

Baudelaire lamented in the nineteenth century that people do not want to talk about what really matters. To the extent that psychoanalysis offers compelling ways of addressing questions about the good life, creative living, love, morality, and spirituality, it will be of continuing interest and importance to people and it will survive.[12] To the extent that it doesn't, people will seek meaning elsewhere—in unencumbered hedonism, material possessions, spiritual quests, gurus, and fundamentalist groups. But I hold out hope for a psychoanalysis that addresses and illuminates these perennial concerns and puts us in touch with what makes us human. Enlarging our being and reanimating the world, such a psychoanalysis offers what culture theorist Raymond Williams termed "resources of hope" for postmodern selves-at-risk.[13]

CHAPTER ONE

PSYCHOANALYSIS AND CREATIVE LIVING

We must not forget that only a very few people are artists in
life; that the art of life is the most distinguished and rarest of
all the arts.

—Jung

CONSIDER THE FOLLOWING VIGNETTE: "He makes her sit down in an
armchair balanced on springs . . . certain levers and gears advance twenty dag-
gers until their points graze her skin; the man frigs himself, the while explaining that the least movement of the chair will cause her to be stabbed."[1] "He" is
in control. He is the "author" or "director" of a scenario that "she" is enslaved
to. He has the freedom to act; she is helpless, trapped, and immobilized. She is
an object-for-the-director's-use, not a subject with her own unique and independent wishes and needs. Any independent action on her part will be literally
deadly for her. This is a *perverse* scenario.

We usually link perversity with sexual activities and practices such as
voyeurism and fetishism, bondage and exhibitionism. But if we consider for a
moment the common ingredients in perverse scenarios, there may be perverse
relationships with people or ideas that are nonsexual. While most perverse scenarios do not have the explicit death threat in the vignette from the Marquis de
Sade's autobiography, they do have an author who is completely in charge and
fashions a reprogrammed, rigid, and stereotypical script. The scene is always
scripted beforehand, invariable, and compulsive. There is no originality. The
author has all the power and implements a unilateral fantasy[2] on a person who

9

is weak and enslaved. "Problems of colonization," as Mannoni usefully reminds us, "did not only concern overseas countries."[3] The people involved in perverse scenarios are psychologically colonized. They are treated by the author/director as things, not people,[4] who have no shaping input on the relationship. They are merely a means, rather than being of ultimate significance themselves. They are *Its* rather than *Thous*, in Buber's sense.

A life of perversity is sterile, devitalized, and impoverished. One remains alienated from other people, whom one tries to control, have power over, and silence. Intimacy cannot grow on such soil. Dominance precludes dialogue. One cannot learn from other people when one has an authoritarian relationship to them.

So if perversity constrains and degrades the human spirit, what expands and elevates it? Creativity, that mysterious and multidimensional expression of originality, beauty and inspiration enlivens and enriches us. Psychoanalysts have been interested in creativity since the inception of psychoanalysis. There are twenty-two references to writings "dealing mainly or largely with Art, Literature or the theory of Aesthetics" in the *Standard Edition* of Freud's work.[5] Freud had a keen appreciation and love of plays, novels, poetry and the visual arts. His writings contain more references to playwrights and novelists, especially Shakespeare and Goethe, than to other psychiatrists. He wrote about *Hamlet*, Dostoevsky, and Michelangelo.

The world of art and of creativity has also been of great interest to many of Freud's contemporaries (e.g., Rank and Jung) and successors (e.g., Kris, Eissler, Winnicott, Milner, Rycroft, McDougall, Rose, Rothenberg, Arieti, Roland, Oremland, Ogden, and Turco, among others). They have attempted to build on and enrich Freud's reflections on the nature of creation and art.

Psychoanalysis may be viewed, as Sheldon Bach aptly notes, as "the opposite of perversion, because in principle it embraces the difficult task of understanding a person, rather than using him, although it, too, can easily enough become a perversion itself."[6]

Let's briefly consider Freud's[7] reflections on creativity and the artist in "Creative Writers and Day-Dreaming," which became paradigmatic for the views of many subsequent psychoanalysts, in light of Bach's[8] cautionary warning about the perverse possibilities in psychoanalysis. The artist, claims Freud, is a neurotic, "oppressed by excessively powerful instinctual needs"; the artist "turns away from reality and transfers all his interest, and his libido too, to the wishful constructions of his life of phantasy, whence the path might lead to neurosis."[9] Furthermore, the artist seeks substitute satisfactions of "honour, power, wealth, fame and the love of women."[10]

Psychoanalysts who have worked with artists in psychoanalytic treatment have clinically observed the way this portrait illuminates a subject that is often idealized and romanticized. For the work of art can be, for example, a form of pathological mourning, in which earlier, formative psychic wounds, injuries, or lacunae are recurrently embodied in the artistic creation, yet not psychologically worked through or transformed. Psychoanalysts have also witnessed the way that the work of art can put the creator in a kind of self-protective, narcissistic cocoon that impedes, if not precludes, availability for intimacy with others.

Freud's analysis of creativity in this essay became received wisdom for many of his successors. Psychoanalytic excursions into art and creativity, with rare exceptions,[11] have all too often been characterized by reductionism and a penchant for pathologization, treating art mostly as a matter of mastering trauma or escaping from reality.[12] Freud's study of Leonardo da Vinci, for example, was called a "pathography" not a biography.[13] Reading the psychoanalytic literature, one gets the distinct impression that art is usually mired in autobiography (never transcending its roots in the artist's personal past) and linked to emotional illness.

But this analysis by Freud—who elsewhere recognized that the artist knew more than was dreamt of in psychoanalytic psychologies[14]—raises more questions than it answers: Is all artistic creation reducible to a single motive? Do artists create for any other purpose than achieving honor, power, wealth, fame, and the love of women? Don't the artistic works that profoundly move us such as the Greek tragedies, the plays of Shakespeare, the symphonies of Mozart, the sculpture of Michelangelo, and the novels of Dostoevsky illuminate rather than evade or escape from reality? While art can fuel neurosis, can it not also be adaptive, aiding the artist (or the audience) in processing, working through, mastering, and even healing disturbing realities?

Psychoanalysis is ambivalent about creativity. On the one hand, it can help artists work through or remove obstacles to the creative process and even elucidate creative products. On the other hand, psychoanalytic treatment of art and artists demonstrates a reductiveness—at times a "perversity"—that is anathema to creativity. Psychoanalysis as a discipline has often viewed itself as a master discourse, the One-Who-Knows the true meaning of art and literature, as well as religion and other complex human creations. From this intellectually imperialistic perspective, art is rarely viewed as a potentially valuable source of enriching knowledge for psychoanalysts. Psychoanalysis, consequently, is impoverished.

When psychoanalysts know too much ahead of time about what an artist's motivations really are or are reducible to, or what a work of art really means, and when art is nothing but an illustration of a psychoanalytic notion, then psychoanalysts may be uncannily enacting a perverse scenario, in which the work of art or the artist is a psychologically silenced and colonized underling in a psychoanalyst's unilateral and reductive scenario about art and creativity. In our highly reactive moral climate, the word "perversion" has an undeniable moral charge attached to it. I am trying to use the word without such conventional, nonpsychoanalytic moral overtones, deliberately taking the liberty of extending the literal meaning of "perversion" in its sexual sense into the metaphoric sense of what might be called "perverse" relationships to artistic creations and ideas as well as people.

While "creative" writers are, as Freud admits, "apt to know a whole host of things between heaven and earth of which our [psychoanalytic] philosophy has not yet let us dream,"[15] all too often psychoanalysts operate as if they have the final answers and the last word on art and artists. Instead of appreciating a work of art on its own merit—allowing a poem or painting to enlighten and enrich them—they often reduce it to an illustration of the thesis that the author had before encountering the creative work. The work of art is a means to the psychoanalyst's egocentric ends. The author "finds" what he or she already believed.

From the eminent art historian Meyer Shapiro who objected to Freud's[16] study of Leonardo to various anthropologists who have challenged the presumed universality of the Oedipus complex, humanists have rejected psychoanalytic interpretations that purport to be comprehensive. But artists as well as humanists all too often fall victim to the mirror-opposite danger to psychoanalytic imperialism and "perversity." If psychoanalysis has too often been guilty of assuming it can and should have the last word on the meaning and status of art, writers or literary theorists can presume that there is nothing new under the Literary Sun. Then it is too easy to confidently claim, as Walter Kendrick does in "Writing the Unconscious," a study of how "literature came at the unconscious before Freud made a science of it,"[17] that E. M. Forster, James Joyce, D. H. Lawrence, and Virginia Woolf "did not need Freud."[18]

One has only to read W. H. Auden's[19] "In Memory of Sigmund Freud" or the letter Virginia Woolf, Thomas Mann, Stefan Zweig, and 192 other writers and artists sent Freud on the occasion of his eightieth birthday hailing him as "the pioneer of a new and deeper knowledge of man," a "courageous seer and healer . . . a guide to hitherto undreamt-of regions of the human soul"[20] to wonder whether Freud (and psychoanalysis) was as unessential to literature as Kendrick contended. And the subsequent artistic movements (e.g., Cubism, Surrealism, Dada, and Abstract Expressionism) and works of literature that draw on psychoanalytic theory and method or that have been shaped by psychoanalytic sensibilities raise crucial questions about the validity of these assertions concerning the limitations of psychoanalysis.

Many artists avoid psychoanalysis, fearing that it is benign at best and corrosive at worst, eroding or inhibiting their creativity by lessening their suffering or questioning their motives. Some artists I have worked with psychoanalytically have voiced this directly, fearing that their creativity would be compromised or diminished by psychoanalytic treatment. Other artists express this less directly. And others, such as the writer Rainer Maria Rilke, never even enter treatment because they believe psychoanalysis will hurt their creativity.

Playwright Arthur Miller illustrates the first kind of concern; author James Agee the third. "In the early fifties," notes Miller, "I realized there was something obsessional in my thoughts about my marriage and my work; great swellings of love and hope for my future with Mary [his wife] were followed by a cycle of despairing resentment that I was being endlessly judged, hopelessly condemned." Attempting to break out of this, Miller sought psychoanalytic treatment. But Miller indicates that he was unable to remain in analysis because of the risk to his creativity. He writes, for example, of his treatment with Rudolph Loewenstein, a "Freudian of great skill, but it was ultimately impossible for me to risk my creativity, which he was wise enough not to pretend to understand, by vacating my own autonomy, however destructive it might continue to be."[21]

James Agee evinced deep interest in and terror of psychoanalysis. He wrote of the agony of his deep, self-destructive tendencies. "I realize that I have an enormously strong drive, on a universally broad front, toward self-destruction . . . I know little if anything about its sources. . . . There is much I might learn and be freed from that causes me and others great pain, frustration and defeat, and I expect that sooner or later I will have to seek their help." But, despite his agony, he avoided psychoanalysis, fearing its impact on him: "Psychiatry, and for that matter psychoanalysis still more, interest me intensely; but except for general talk with them—which I would like—I feel reluctant to use either except in really desperate need. . . . But I would somewhere near as soon die (or enter a narcotic world) as undergo a full psychoanalysis . . . I see in every psychoanalyzed face a look of deep spiritual humiliation or defeat; to which I prefer at least a painful degree of spiritual pain and sickness. The look of 'I am a man who finally cannot call his soul his own, but yielded to another.'"[22]

Contrary to Miller and Agee's contentions, in my practice I have experienced the way psychoanalysis can actually help an artist's creativity, rather than threaten it. Interferences to creativity, at one time or another, afflict every artist (as well as every psychoanalyst). Despite the fact that creative products are deeply cherished and keenly awaited by their creators, they are frequently avoided or postponed. Procrastination and inhibitions undermine even the most promising project. Psychoanalysis can foster the creativity of artists in treatment by illuminating and elucidating the psychological obstacles to it. Psychopathology, according to Mitchell, leads to a "failure of imagination,"[23] that is, a tendency to relate to self, others, and the world in old and restrictive ways. Studying the way psychopathology hinders creativity could, in certain times of creative blockage, be illuminating for artists. Psychoanalytic authors have documented a range of factors that interfere with the creative process.

Let's briefly consider several. Creativity can be self-destabilizing as well as self-enriching. Certain artists who cannot "modulate excitement (and/or tension)" can avoid the "risk of overstimulation" by renouncing artistic experiences that are excessively stimulating.[24] Success, as well as pathology, can impede creativity, predisposing an artist to utilize a style or subject matter that "works," instead of risking new ventures with uncertain results. Otto Rank stressed the guilt triggered by one's creativity and individuation.[25] The artist's success and acclaim may threaten colleagues and friends. Fearing aloneness, we inhibit our creativity in order to remain connected to less creative family members and peers. The artist's conscious or unconscious allegiance to these relationships may also endanger creativity, generating fear about exploring new vistas and thereby threatening the fabric of established relationships. Psychoanalytic authors have also illuminated other factors that impede creativity, including fear of "aloneness,"[26] the way society favors male artists, and the demands on women artists of procreation and parenting. Analysts have also elucidated the way noncongenial familial environments, as well as individual and societal dynamics, can inhibit creativity. In certain families with excessively utilitarian value systems and practical goals, artistic children are deeply discouraged from pursuing their artistic passion and their inchoate creative efforts are never appreciated or affirmed. Creativity has trouble sprouting from this soil.

In *Tales from the Couch: Writers on Therapy*, a wide range of novelists, poets, essayists, and nonfiction writers—including George Plimpton, Ntozake Shange, Adam Gopnik, Phillip Lopate, Diane Ackerman, Mark Doty, Susan Cheever, and Emily Fox Gordon—explore the myriad benefits of therapy for writers. These and other authors stress the way therapy cultivated increased self-awareness and self-trust, fostered greater candor and freedom, and stimulated an understanding of the creative process and renewed passion for their own creative efforts. "Psychoanalysis has made me a finer writer and a fuller person" writes Ntozake Shange. "Through the language of psychoanalysis I have learned—am always learning," says Susan Wood, "to speak my own language, the idiom of who I have been, who I am and who I will be, and to be comfortable with, even relish, the unknowable mystery of the self." "In my life successful therapy gave birth to successful writing," writes Rebecca Walker.[27]

The commonly held belief among many artists that psychoanalysis will stifle their creativity misses the potentially creative role it might play in enhancing, rather than eroding or inhibiting it. But this can only happen if psychoanalysts work through their own ambivalence about creativity and their tendency to pathologize it. Otherwise, psychoanalysis will treat works of art as nothing but evidence for the pathography of the artist.

Still, it is not enough to rescue creativity from psychoanalysts who unwittingly 'shrink' it. Wresting creativity from the "psychopathological cast that it tends to assume in psychoanalytic writings" is a necessary, but insufficient project.[28] We also must work through the perversity that has haunted psychoanalytic excursions into the artistic realm. "Art must always say 'and yet!' to life," Georg Lukács writes. When psychoanalytic examinations of art generate interpretations that offer no new perspectives on life and living because they find what they already believe before they even encounter the work of art, then no matter how incisive and sophisticated these analyses seem, painters, poets, and novelists will continue to be psychologically colonized by psychoanalysts even when their art is no longer overtly pathologized. Psychoanalysis will then be devitalized.

Why are we perverse and what can we do about it? In my clinical experience, perversions are often a substitute for something emotionally vital that is missing (George Atwood, personal communication, 1998)—namely, intimacy that is self-enriching rather than self-annihilating. Perversions also represent an attempt at self-healing of earlier trauma. Perversions often enact or defend one against the reexperiencing of exploitative, dissociated relationships in the past, by which I mean interactions that were traumatic and are repressed and often repeated in present relationships.

Perverse relations can also be seen as an attempt to create an environment of safety and satisfaction that banishes the anxiety of intimacy or exploitation. Self-vulnerability and enormous deprivation are warded off as one relates to others in the exploitative (or submissive) manner that one experienced with significant people in one's past. This can take two forms: adopting a position of dominance so that one is not controlled and exploited, or subservience so that one "identifies with the aggressor" and thereby aligns oneself with the world of the dominator. In either scenario, nonperverse relationships open up the deadly specter of profound betrayal and the eradication or the extreme diminishment of the integrity of one's experience of self. Although perverse relations lead to personal and interpersonal impoverishment, they may keep at bay horrendous experiences of self-loss or self-humiliation that one may not even remember, even as one continues to lead a life that reenacts such perverse connections with others.

Perversions ward off existential as well as psychological dangers. Animals are born with the instinctual equipment they need to survive in their world. But humans do not fit so seamlessly into their environments. The "intrauterine existence" of the human infant, according to Freudian anthropology, "seems to be short in comparison with that of most animals." Humans are "sent out into the world in a less finished" and therefore more helpless "state" than the young of other species.[29] The "unfinished" character of the human organism at birth, what Gehlen terms our "instinctual deprivation,"[30] the fact that our biological equipment does not match the demands of embodied, mortal existence, leaves us in a precarious ontological position. In addition, we are capable of raising questions about our existence and fate that we fundamentally cannot answer: "Why are we born?" "What is the purpose of our existence?" "Why are we mortal?" Humans seem to be the only species that can contemplate its own eventual and inevitable demise. We humans confront an unbearable complexity and heaviness of being; we are impotent in the face of the awesomeness of the universe, the reality of finitude and the uncontrollableness of others. Perversion may be related to what Ernest Becker[31] terms *fetishism*, a conscious narrowing down of our reality. Perversions are safer than the agonizing immensity of freedom. Freedom is terrifying for a creature without a map, sailing to a destination—death—that it cannot fathom or tolerate. Perverse relations are a way of taming the terror of mortal, embodied existence by denying and reducing the overwhelmingness of reality and our own all-too-human vulnerability and helplessness.[32] When psychoanalysis has a nonperverse relationship to the imagination, then its latent capacity to enrich creative living may emerge.

Creativity is complex and multidimensional. The musical originality of Mozart, the literary inventiveness of Shakespeare, and the resourceful statesmanship (and capacity to foster social change) of Mahatma Gandhi and Martin Luther King Jr. are all different. Musicians, visual artists, scientists, religious innovators, psychoanalysts, and leaders in the civic arena can all be creative.

To be creative is to have a receptivity to oneself and the world, a great pleasure in exercising one's capacities, an internal openness and flexibility, an attraction to novelty, a sensitivity to discrepant perceptions and observations (John Keats's "negative capability"), an alertness to seize new opportunities, the courage to challenge traditions and conventions, the capacity to integrate apparent opposites (Jung's enantiodromia), and the ability to imagine and devise new approaches to a problem or question by bringing together two previously separate and segregated frameworks in a new and fruitful way.

Such Janusian thinking[33] generates new and surprising combinations. This will result in giving form to something novel and valuable through a deliberate (albeit unself-conscious and self-forgetful) process culminating in such things as a work of art, a new way of relating to the world, a novel career, an original style of parenting, or a unique plan for enhancing international peace.

People go to psychoanalysts for many conscious and unconscious reasons, including resolving disturbing symptoms, working out personal or interpersonal inhibitions, and freeing up the capacity to enjoy life and to love. But can psychoanalysis contribute to the art of creative living?

Creativity doesn't just occur in museums, concert halls, or jazz clubs. It can also happen in everyday life.[34] There is, as Jung aptly noted, an "art" of living.[35] Although one does not ordinarily associate going to a psychoanalyst with living more creatively, in this concluding section of the chapter I will briefly discuss how psychoanalysis could foster more creative living.

DREAMING INTO LIFE

We are such stuff as dreams are made on.
—Shakespeare

We seem to know more about what creativity is than how to facilitate it. "'To make someone love the unconscious, *that*, is teaching art,'" Anton Ehrenzweig once said to Marion Milner.[36] In a good-enough psychoanalysis one experiences a deep respect for dreaming and unconsciousness, which may be one important, and unexpected, way of fostering human creativity.

Freud's description of the dreamwork—the way experiences preceding the dream ("day residues") link up with unresolved emotional conflicts from the past to form the nighttime dream composed of condensed and displaced images—affords a doorway into the creativity of the psyche.[37] "Freud democratized genius," as Phillip Rieff evocatively noted, "by giving everyone a creative unconscious."[38] Our capacity to dream demonstrates that all of us—not just the economically privileged or the intellectually talented—are more creative than we imagine.[39] Before Freud, Jung, and their psychoanalytic colleagues and successors, the psyche was seen and understood in more mechanical, flattened, and impoverished ways. Freud and Jung revealed that experience is usually more symbolic, imaginal, fertile, and complex than it seems, and that actions often have multiple meanings and purposes.

The creative status Freud bestowed on art in his less reductionistic moments was most fully explored and illuminated in dreams, art, mythology, and other imaginal forms by Jung and his followers. Viewing the unconscious as a seedbed of creativity, not simply a Pandora's box, Jung "depathologized" the psyche.[40] He widened the value of dreams by finding other meanings besides revelations of infantile reminiscences and disguised sexuality. Jung's "synthetic-constructive" approach toward interpretation of psychic activity, his emphasis on the goal or purpose of emotional life rather than simply its cause or source, complements Freud's analytic-genetic approach, his focus on reducing experience into its component parts (such as wishing and striving) and tracing its historical origins in infantile childhood experience and its antecedent causes.[41] Jung saw the constructive method as complementary to the reductive method of classical psychoanalysis: "We apply a reductive point of view in all cases where it is a question of illusions, fictions, and exaggerated attitudes. On the other hand, a constructive point of view must be considered for all cases where the conscious attitude is more or less normal, but capable of greater development and refinement, or where unconscious tendencies, also capable of development, are being misunderstood and kept under by the conscious mind."[42]

Jung emphasized that the psyche is "prospective" or purposive, self-regulating, self-healing,[43] and oriented toward the present and the future, as well as profoundly shaped by formative experiences in the past. "No psychological fact can ever be explained in terms of causality alone" claims Jung,[44] "as a living phenomenon, it is always indissolubly bound up with the continuity of the vital process, so that it is not only something evolved but also continually evolving and creative."[45] Jung was interested in elaborating the forward-moving direction of contemporaneous phenomena such as dreams and then integrating them into one's life as well as tracing their historical antecedents. "I use constructive and synthetic to designate a method that is the antithesis of reductive. The constructive method is concerned with the elaboration of the products of the unconscious (dreams, fantasies, etc.). It takes an unconscious product as a symbolic expression which anticipates a coming phase of psychological development."[46]

Jung's "wisdom of the psyche" has been correctly critiqued for neglecting the tragic dimensions of human existence and sometimes being too teleological (Don Kalshed, personal communication, 1999). But it provides an important antidote to Freud's pathologizing of mental life. A prospective approach explores the positive functions a symptom or dream provides in a person's life. It asks a different sort of question such as "What is this symptom for?" rather than "What does the symptom hide or evade?" A prospective approach can amplify the new possibilities a dream or symptom points to in one's present and future, as well as what imaginal phenomena mean.

A crucial and perhaps neglected implication of Freud's insights about dreaming is that the dreaming experience is not something that happens only in sleep. Freud implies a link between dreams and daily life when he writes: "The latent thoughts of the dream differ in no respect from the products of our regular conscious activity."[47] The dreaming experience and imaginal and unconscious phenomena are happening all the time in waking life as a relatively silent yet influential backdrop to our conscious secondary process experience. Most people, however, treat nocturnal dreaming as more crucial. The transformative potential of the dreaming experience is thus perhaps insufficiently appreciated and inadvertently segregated from our waking consciousness.

The dreaming experience is applicable to daily life. Think of the dream as a model for the unconscious operation of thought in daily life—the way that experiences during the day, like dreams, contain condensed and displaced symbols and hidden meanings triggered by some instigating force in our experience that can aid in self-understanding and self-healing. Unconscious facets of our experience are encouraged to emerge when we relate to experiences in daily life in the uniquely creative way that Freud and Jung, among others, taught us to play with dreams. Freud recommended listening to and speaking about dreams with that meditative state of mind he termed "evenly-hovering attention" and "free association."[48] Jung advocated, in his writings on "active imagination,"[49] that we amplify the meaning and resonance of the images through painting, drawing, sculpting, dancing, or singing. Then the world of daily life—sights and sounds, images and ideas in novels or movies, the art in our homes and offices, the people we converse with, the plays and music that move us, the sensuous pleasures we relish, soft reveries, roaring fantasies, quiet or noisy somatizations, passions, or addictions—contain unsuspected meanings. They may be triggers of or sites for condensed or displaced images and meanings that reveal the hopes and dreams, terrors and untapped potentials of their creators. Bollas, in a felicitous phrase, terms this process the "dream work of one's life."[50]

Art can be an "externalized dream"[51] as the films of Federico Fellini illustrate, containing symbols and meanings that exceed what the creator knew or intended to convey. An artist I once worked with in psychoanalytic treatment—call him Donald—initiated therapy because of a vague and diffuse sense of pain. He experienced himself as worthless and strange, which he described during the initial stages of therapy, in an ill-defined and general way. I knew from what he reported that he believed his parents viewed him as despicable and that he had felt deeply condemned by them and powerless in their presence. After about a year of therapy he had a memory of sketching, many years before, a dwarf that represented, for him, "all he hated of himself condensed into one figure." His body. His feeling of being emotionally weird. His conviction of insignificance. His parents' wholesale condemnation of his being. The drawing and his associations to it revealed an unconscious self-image that had haunted him his whole life and eluded representation and thus transformation. Once the image, and the accompanying feelings of self-loathing and alienation emerged, the therapy proceeded on a deeper and more productive level.

The dreamwork of daily life occurs not only when we create a work of art, but also in what we are drawn to, which may include more prosaic examples in addition to art. Exploring the meaning of symbols in art and life, as well as in dreams, reveals unsuspected creative potentials in our lives. A man on a vacation, a therapist who has finished his psychoanalysis, is deeply drawn to a sculpture on a wall in an open storage room in the back of a local art gallery. The sculpture, entitled Triptych, is composed of three narrow pieces of dark bronze, side by side, part of a face with eyes either closed or sightless, bursting through the center of each strip. After he returned to the gallery three times in the same week to see the sculpture he became curious about the source of his fascination. Although he loves art, this kind of enthrallment is unusual for him. He didn't dream the sculpture. It was obviously something real that captured his attention and imagination. But exploring the meaning for him of the fractured faces, like an image in a dream, opened up new dimensions of himself.

He eventually realized that to survive the deadening atmosphere in his family, where talk about things and accomplishments substituted for the sharing of feelings, he developed passions and interests—such as art and soccer—outside of his critical and intrusive parents' sphere of influence and control. Then his hobbies could be protected from being stolen or colonized by his parents. As a result, he was composed of several hidden and divided tributaries that did not flow into one main body of self. He felt internally at odds and pulled in too many directions. Triptych, the sculpture of one face fractured into three, each struggling to emerge, represented three fragments or faces of himself—the athlete, the healer, and the artist—that needed to be united into a single whole. Seeing such a concrete representation of his deepest self in the sculpture made the fissures in himself much clearer and more obvious.

The world has a hidden richness of a dream when we are willing to play with and decode it. Overdetermined, emotionally charged, condensed, and displaced images that symbolically encode unresolved emotional conflicts and unrealized potentials from the past are evoked by experiences in the present. As we develop the capacity to play with and associate to these images in an unfettered way, a variety of further meanings emerge and point in unpredictable directions. New insights, questions, pathways, and dreams are generated by our conscious reflection on and interpretation of these evocative trains of thought and emotion. Our capacity to engage in the dreamwork of our lives may lie fallow for a while until an experience in the present triggers new condensed and displaced images resplendent with evocative possibilities, which we then decode in our unique way.

The external as well as the internal environment can be reanimated when we are attuned to the dreamwork of our lives. A woman drives through a parking lot behind a small shopping center to humor her son, an in-line skating and skateboard enthusiast. He looks quite content. She is bored. As she drives around the garbage cans, torn railings, and steps at the back of the shopping center she asks him why he wanted to go there. "You are not looking at this place as a skater would," he informed her, as he noticed that the rail, fire hydrant, staircase, and ledge were a challenging and compelling course for a skateboarder.

Psychoanalysis cultivates the capacity to dream by day as well as by night and thus to treat the world as what Winnicott termed a potential space in which people, one's own history, nature, objects, and experiences can be imaginatively engaged and reanimated. Winnicott's writings on playing, creativity, and potential and transitional space add an important dimension to Freud and Jung's views of dreaming and unconsciousness by contextualizing and interpersonalizing them.[52] Winnicott places the dream and unconscious mentation in transitional space. We ordinarily divide the world into two: the world outside ourselves and the world within. Winnicott wrote about a third zone of being, an intermediate or transitional space in which creativity (and, I will argue in a later chapter, spirituality) occur. This transitional space is neither inside nor outside but partakes of both. It draws on but is not reducible to either. It is in this intermediate zone of experience that dreaming, creativity, and creative living occurs. Winnicott teaches us that creativity is not a possession of a solitary individual but a process generated by a creative relation between a person who is internally receptive and an outer world that often includes another person.

The inner attitude of openness to the outer world, to surprise, to wonder, to people and to feedback enlarges rather than compresses psychic and interpersonal space. One approaches life and relationships in an alive, fresh, and vital way. There is more fluid communication between conscious and unconscious dimensions of ourselves. In creative moments, a person, like a sail, can be moved by the winds of life. One can be influenced or transformed by the feedback of others and one's plans and direction can change in the moment. One questions inherited and conventional assumptions and practices, one makes novel connections—integrating two things that were formerly separate—and one imagines the currently unimaginable.

When psychic space is uncongealed, we can comprehend and tolerate complexity, ambiguity, and multidimensionality in ourselves, other people, and the world. Most of us are ontological dualists; we divide the world into innumerable sets of oppositions such as self and other, altruism and self-care, and mind and body, and so forth. We ordinarily treat such facets of being as separate and opposed. We favor one and neglect the other. Self-care becomes more important than altruism or the mind is more valued than the body. When psychic space is enlarged, apparent dichotomies and oppositions that ordinarily limit creative living are treated as interpenetrating and potentially enriching facets of being. Living beyond such dualisms affords a fuller and more fertile life. The capacity to make novel connections between spheres of our existence that are ordinarily separated and segregated is thereby intensified and enhanced. New ways of being can be actualized. The world may thus be reenchanted and reanimated. As differences and otherness in oneself and others are more accepted and valued, empathy for self and others is deepened.

Being an artist of one's life is thrilling but difficult. Dreaming and the creativity it fosters are "murdered" in certain people.[53] They cannot imagine, dream, or play. Imaginativeness is precluded if not foreclosed when we are too moored and mired in concrete reality or too lost in obsessive ruminations or fantasying. Our inner psychic life then resembles a frozen tundra or a broken record more than a free-flowing river.

We impinge on social space, suggests Masud Khan, if we do not use our dream space. Not being able to use our dream space for the dreaming experience, we exploit social space and personal relationships to act out our dreams.[54] Let me mention three ways I believe we do this. Each inhibits creative living.

1. Everyday thinking reduces, dichotomies, and essentializes; the world of dreaming respects complexity, multidimensionality, and ambiguity. The complexity of the world is eclipsed as we unreflectively divide the world into polar oppositions (e.g., good and evil and spiritual and profane). As we choose sides between them, we create false dichotomies, eclipse the interconnected nature of these apparent dualities, and neglect those facets of experiences that we have devalued.

2. Most of us follow Shakespeare's recommendation in *Hamlet* ("to thine own self be true") and seek our essential, singular essence. But our actual experience of identity in the world teaches us that the bard should have said "to thine own *selves* be true." The multidimensionality of our identities is reduced as we search for our

sole, authentic essence. This predisposes us to neglect certain important facets of our being.[55]

3. The third result of our constrained capacity to dream in daily life is that we dissociate from actual living by fantasying rather than imagining or dreaming.[56] In imagination and dreaming there is a creative engagement and reanimation of the world rather than an escape from it. Think of the adolescent in the parking lot. Fantasying, in Winnicott's sense of the term, is a dissociated, isolating, non-symbolic activity "absorbing energy but not contributing-in either to dreaming or to living."[57] It is a type of daydreaming that has "no poetic value,"[58] by which he means it is repetitive, static, concrete, and cannot be symbolically elaborated: "a dog is a dog is a dog."[59] Fantasying is illustrated by a woman in analysis who is unexcited by her loyal and loving husband and holds out hope without any evidence that a twenty-year-old affair with a man who is not willing to commit to her will one day lead to marriage. Fantasying is unconstructive because it restricts if not paralyzes action and creative living as we remain entrapped within a personally constructed prison of feelings, fantasies, and relationships that remain virtual potentials but are divorced from contact with the world or our lives. Our lives are impoverished when fantasying takes precedence over imagination.

The second major obstacle to being the artists of our own lives is the neurotic, uncreative way that most of us have attempted to heal ourselves of our childhood wounds. Our lives, from this perspective, are the compromised form that our efforts to cure ourselves of our childhood conflicts and illnesses take. Such emotional self-splinting or psychological self-medicating are our own best effort at self-cure. But they lead, even in the best of cases, to a failure of imagination and restrictive, uncreative living.

Psychoanalysis can transform the patient's "practice of self-cure,"[60] the old ways one has attempted to resolve one's core conflicts or developmental arrests and heal oneself. New ways of being and living emerge. A crucial aspect of doing this and appropriating our histories involves what I have termed "self-creation" in the present.[61] Self-creation refers, not to creating ourselves without constraints, which as psychoanalysts we know is impossible, but, rather, to building a personally authentic and meaningful life in the present by creatively reworking and transforming our experience. Such a life is neither a sterile imitation of another's existence, nor a reactive rebellion against ways of living that we may in fact value, but a life that has texture, vitality, and depth and feels creative and alive and authentically one's own. Unsuspected ways of relating to ourselves and others emerge.

I have stressed dreaming and imagination as crucial components of creative living. Another crucial aspect is the style and form of our lives.[62] In a good-enough psychoanalysis, one finds one's own unique voice/way of being, which is an essential precondition of creative living. Personal idiom is the unique nucleus or kernel that is us and that can, under favorable circumstances, evolve and unfold.[63] It is our unique aesthetic sensibility and the idiosyncratic form and rhythm that each of us is. In her moving poem, "When Death Comes," Mary Oliver writes: "When it's over, I don't want to wonder/if I have made of my life something particular and real./ . . . I don't want to end up simply having visited the world."[64] We are all unique complexities—as different in our being as our fingerprints or faces—with inimitable brushstrokes that we (each individually) can potentially contribute to the canvass of life.

We live our uniqueness not by discovering a blueprint from our past that tells us how to live, but by finding and playing with the unique set of dispositions and possibilities and unknown and emerging potentials that are ours alone. Some may be more explicit, like our unique view of the world, or the cultural and sensuous pleasures we enjoy. Other facets can be subtler, like our unique dreams, the meaning of the art on our walls, the artifacts on our desks, or the rhythm of our being.

Psychoanalysis began as improvisation. The early analysts were playing mental jazz without too much psychological sheet music. As psychoanalysis became more codified, it aspired to be a science more than an art and was more systematized and routinized. That psychoanalysts are still hypnotized by the image of the psychoanalyst as scientist emerges in the unproductive debates about whether psychoanalysis is or is not a science. Defenders of psychoanalysis, from my perspective, are more revealing on this score than attackers. While the former defend psychoanalysis against externalized enemies (e.g., those critics such as Adolph Grunbaum who critique psychoanalysis for not being a science), they reveal an unconscious allegiance to science by accepting the problematic premise of their critics—namely, that psychoanalysis should be a science and is fundamentally weakened if it is not.

We analysts often unconsciously view ourselves as "customs officials" who make sure that "the rules are followed and that nothing foreign/illegal is smuggled in."[65] When the analyst is viewed more as artist than scientist, for example, as a jazz improviser who has a great deal of knowledge about the fundamentals of human development, mental functioning, and the analytic relationship and process, but improvises in therapy depending on the exigencies of the moment, then art and imagination may take on greater importance in understanding and elucidating the analyst's functioning, and thereby enrich the analytic experience for both patient and analyst.

Creativity is essential to human life. It is crucial to the health of both individuals and the larger society. Cultures and people need novelty and innovation in modes of thinking and living in order to reach their potential. Many of the problems confronting us as individuals and as a culture could be more successfully addressed, and even resolved, if they were approached freshly and creatively.

To the extent that psychoanalysis fears its own unruly creativity by resisting its own most fertile and radical insights about unconsciousness and dream mentation, it will become fossilized and probably be viewed by more and more people as a historical remnant of a bygone age. To the extent that psychoanalysis remains open to its own unpredictable generativeness by eluding its own perverse tendencies, continually questioning its own insights, remaining open to feedback about its limits, learning from its own most emancipatory discoveries, to the extent that psychoanalysis is a ceaseless, unguarded opening that keeps expanding, it will speak to the needs of people in the twentieth-first century who will be enriched by the creativity it fosters.[66]

CHAPTER TWO

VALUES AND ETHICS IN PSYCHOANALYSIS

To know who you are is to be oriented in moral space, a space in which questions arise about what is good or bad, what is worth doing and what not, what has meaning and importance for you and what is trivial and secondary.

—Charles Taylor

A PATIENT, WHOM I WILL CALL HAROLD, begins a session by telling me that he has finally been able to raise his consulting fees. His tone is upbeat and triumphant. He has struggled with this for a long time, feeling that he does not "deserve" it. Raising his fee represents, for him, a new and tenuous capacity to care for himself. Respecting himself was not something that was encouraged when he was growing up. As the "fireman" in his chaotic and abusive family, he was/is constantly called on to put out the family blazes. There was little or no concern for his own feelings or needs. Constantly berated by his highly critical father, he doubts his abilities, feels wracked by free-floating guilt, and neglects himself as he accommodates to the needs of others. In the course of our work together we have witnessed many occasions in which he has habitually put the needs of others first and completely neglected his own.

Typically feeling deprived and depleted, he experienced changing his fee as an inchoate sign of a newly developing and fragile self-respect. I did too. But as the session unfolded I had other, discrepant feelings. I first became aware of these feelings when he indicated that he was "just going to raise his fee" without saying anything to his clients. If any clients objected, he would ask them if

25

they had "received the letter that I sent you." He indicated that he had never sent such a letter nor did he ever intend to. I was struck by his unself-conscious tone and his seeming obliviousness to his clients. I knew from previous discussions about his subsequent guilt over mistreating his wife when she "made a mistake" (like not putting a stamp on an envelope) that he had great difficulty empathizing with perspectives other than his own, periodically treating people like his father treated him. To even conceive of the validity of other perspectives felt like he was giving up and handing over his reality to them. As I remembered Harold's remorse in the past over the way his wife "had been more there for me than I had been there for her," my sense of his life kaleidoscopically shifted. I recognized that his fee change was shaped, at least in part, by his fear of confrontation and disappointment and his consequent need to do an end run around potentially disturbing interpersonal interactions. I also realized that life, for him, was not simply a tale of the way others had deprived and depleted him, but might also include the way he, like his father, often treated others as mere objects in his quest to get what he 'needed.' Many questions arose for me about his fee change as I reflected on these two ways of seeing his life. Did what he was doing trouble him in any way? Would he like to be treated the way he was treating his clients? Would there be a value in exploring his diminished capacity for what Benjamin terms "mutual recognition,"[1] the ability to see the other as a *subject* with his or her own unique ideals, desires, and needs, not simply as an object-for-the-self's-use? Was he "beating his clients to the punch" so that he would not be vulnerable and exploited the way he had felt with his father? How might therapists respond when a patient's self-actualizing behavior hurts others? What does a therapist do in the face of unethical or duplicitous behavior?

Values and morality play a subtle and important role in the analytic process. While many analysts may claim that values have no place in the analytic enterprise, one of the sociological realities of contemporary psychoanalytic practice is that with the ascendance of our 'psychological' society, psychoanalysts are asked to address value and moral questions that formerly were the province only of religion.[2] During the time I have been working on this chapter, patients have raised the following questions: How should one respond to the immorality of co-workers? Should one leave a "bad" (= depriving) marriage and "hurt" one's children? Should a child have contact with a deadbeat Dad? Is a cybersex affair a betrayal of one's spouse?

But of course psychoanalysis, like any human enterprise, is permeated by values. Let me give two examples. The analytic relationship is based on the assumption that the analyst's "analytic attitude" toward the patient of single-minded interest, attentiveness, empathy, and nondefensiveness is a constructive, helpful way of being. But there are untoward, as well as positive, consequences to these values that rarely seem to be explored. I have repeatedly witnessed, for example, the way the therapeutic relationship can foster unrealistic narcissistic expectations in patients about a quality of therapeutic devotion and attunement in relationships outside treatment with spouses, friends, or colleagues that unnecessarily burdens those relationships.

Second, values underlie the analyst's conceptions of mental health, about the kind of life worth living, that shape the analyst's sense of what a person is and should be. An analyst influenced by a Freudian vision will tend to value a renunciate ethics of austerity (giving up irrational childhood longing and wishes) more that a hedonistic morality of self-gratification or a redemptive religious worldview. A therapist in a more collectivist culture than the United States might question, rather than take for granted, the value of individuation and self-reliance that is so highly valued in many parts of Western culture. Conceptions of values guide (if not circumscribe) the analyst's way of viewing the treatment and relating to the patient. Psychoanalysts have insufficiently examined questions related to the values underlying their images of mental health and the aims or ends of treatment. And these hidden values deeply affect the clinical encounter. There are important clinical consequences depending on whether an analyst believes, as Freud did, that the best humans can do is attain "common unhappiness,"[3] or whether an analyst maintains, as Fromm did, that humans are capable of "well-being," which entails not simply the "absence of illness," but the "presence of well-being"[4]: being fully born, overcoming narrow views of the self, being completely aware of and responsive to the world.

In a psychoanalysis that reflected more actively on the hidden values that shape its conception of the good life new questions might more readily become available: What is the impact on treatment and the patient of psychoanalysis being essentially a psychology of illness?[5] How would treatment be transformed if psychoanalysis did not neglect a psychology of health? Does psychoanalysis ever promote adjustment to a deranged world?

There seems to be a tension and ambivalence within psychoanalysis concerning this topic. On the one hand, many analysts still seem to aspire to being 'scientific' and believe that values have no place in psychoanalysis. They are echoing Freud's[6] claim that psychoanalysis does not posit any values beyond those within science as a whole. On the other hand, despite the supposed neutrality of psychoanalysis, moral questions pervade it from the implicit and explicit values in our theories and practices to the value dilemmas of our patients.

Not only are psychoanalysts asked to address moral issues, it is imperative that they do so. For we are living, as I suggested in the Introduction, in a highly amoral age. There is moral anarchy in most, if not all, sectors of American life. Governmental officials, CEOs, and religious leaders are embroiled in ethical scandals. Getting what one "needs" (an unconscious narcissistic translation of what one "wants") guides the actions of too many people. There is scant moral accountability. Hedonism and instant gratification permeate American culture.

The moral shallowness and malaise characterizing our culture all too often generate two narrow responses: a politics of piousness and blame or a culture of victimization and complaint, by which I mean that we either vilify individuals who engage in unscrupulous behavior without understanding the context of their lives or their actions (expecting them to toe a moral line that we draw and may cross ourselves) or we disclaim moral accountability because of supposedly mitigating psychological or sociological realities ("The Menendez brothers killed their parents because they were abused"), which, of course leaves unanswered the question of why other people in compatible dire circumstances manage to behave morally.

Psychoanalysis could potentially play an important role in responding to the moral shallowness we are mired in as a culture. Understanding unconscious motivations opens up a new dimension for ethical inquiry.[7] Psychoanalysis has the potential to offer a more nuanced moral perspective than contemporary accounts tend to, what I have termed "compassionate accountability,"[8] because it acknowledges the psychological factors underlying amorality without jettisoning moral responsibility. By illuminating motivational complexity, including hidden intentions and unconscious reasons for our actions, psychoanalysis's compassionate accountability could provide a useful resource in contemporary discourse on morality.

Psychoanalysis's stance toward values both helps and hinders us from exploring these and related kinds of issues. The self-reflexive dialogue between analyst and patient provides a context in which questions of values and morality can readily emerge and be explored. In actually bringing more reason to bear on one's asocial, self-centered drivenness and lessening irrational conscience, psychoanalysis can improve our standard of conduct.[9] But, while psychoanalysis may now be very far from Heinz Hartmann's[10] assertion that it is a clinical procedure without moral considerations, the legacy of neutrality also hinders our capacity to reflect on questions of ethics. Therapists are never completely objective. They shape the treatment in subtle and manifold ways. Sometimes these influences are benign; other times they are not. The ideal of impartiality is, at its best, an attempt to reduce the possibility of coercive influences. The valuing of neutrality has, unfortunately, created a disciplinary self-image that encourages a phobic attitude toward values, an avoidance of investigating the therapist's impact in this area that compromises the ability of analysts to detect where values secretly shape and restrict the analytic relationship. The ethics of neutrality ironically keeps important material such as politics and morality out of the treatment. The claim that psychotherapy "is an apolitical, amoral practice is itself a political act," notes Cushman.[11] It is a political act in the following ways: It reflects and reproduces contemporary moral and political arrangements, visions of self, and the status quo. It also hides the exercise of power.

There is a great resistance to conceiving of therapy as moral and political. We do not like to think of our work in this way. Psychoanalysts are professionally socialized to view their discipline as a neutral science. It violates our self-images as purveyors of objective, rational Truth to admit that our work is permeated with values. Because psychoanalysis is saturated with values the analyst is inevitably cast into a moral role. "The analyst cannot be merely a neutral investigator of the patient's internal life or an empathic servant of the patient's true self," notes Irwin Hoffman. "Because the patient's experience is multifaceted, intrinsically ambiguous in many ways, and partially opaque, it does not serve up 'data' that can simply be followed as guides to understanding and action. It cannot preempt the analyst's involvement as a moral authority and coconstructor of the reality of the patient's experience. The analyst functions not only as a source of general affirmation but also as a moral influence in relation to the patient's specific choices."[12]

Believing that we should be "neutral" about values, many analysts tend not to look for or see where they are unconsciously operative. It is very difficult to discover what we don't look for (because we don't think that it should be there). This renders unconscious the shaping role of the values that inform the analytic encounter. Not only does the scientific attitude hinder the exploration of values, it cannot guide us from *is* to *ought*; that is, it does not provide any guidance or direction for how to live (James Jones, personal communication, 1997).

Two traditions have dominated how psychoanalysts have addressed questions of values and morality: classical Freudian analysis and postclassical developmental arrest models influenced by Winnicott and Kohut. These perspectives shape how analysts experience and relate to questions of value and morality that arise in treatment. Before describing and examining each, it is important to emphasize that, technically speaking, there is no such thing as "classical psychoanalysis" or Winnicottian/Kohutian analysis. There are only classical analyses and Winnicottian and Kohutian analyses—each different and unique.

Intellectual generalizations are often highly suspect in our postmodern climate, in which such systematic thinking is frowned upon and viewed as reductionistic. Clearly generalizations run the risk of reducing and distorting a complex body of thinking and practice. But generalizations can also highlight trends that we benefit from delineating and articulating. There are important patterns that are eclipsed if we only speak in "local" narratives.

Despite the fact that there are a multitude of ways of thinking and practicing within each school of psychoanalysis, there are particular flavors and predilections in each that differentiate them from other schools of thought and practice. It is in this spirit—in which I realize there are exceptions to my general remarks—that I will generalize about classical, Winnicottian/Kohutian, and interpersonal analysis.

The classical perspective arose during the early days of psychoanalysis and still persists in certain facets of contemporary analysis. From this perspective, patients, like the self-deceived person in Plato's archetypal cave, mistake illusions for Reality. When patients' distortions about self and reality are peeled away and their archaic wishes and illusions are renounced, they will no longer mistake shadows for substance. In this Platonically informed (inspired?) classical Freudian vision, what Kohut called a "truth morality," accurate perception and alignment with the Real will guide one's moral deliberations (Peter Carnochan, personal communication, 1997).[13]

In recent years, another perspective has shaped psychoanalytic deliberations about how to live. From this viewpoint, patients are damaged by the absence of attuned responsiveness or interpersonal impingements from caregivers. Patients develop a compensatory overlay—what Winnicott termed a "false self"—to protect against retraumatization. In this Rousseauian-inspired, developmental arrest model of Winnicott and Kohut, when patients access their buried, hidden authentic Self (rather than Reality), a natural and uncorrupted developmental process will resume. Connecting with either an authentic self underneath a distorting overlay of impingements and/or trauma, compliance and inauthenticity (Winnicott), or a "blueprint" of themselves[14] will provide direction for how to live. Elsewhere[15] I have raised questions about both ways of thinking about identity. Although there is evidence that both Winnicott and Kohut clinically appreciated the complexity of identity, their *theories* of selfhood (the essentialistic True Self and the dualistic bipolar self) tended to reduce it. This predisposes one to clinically *singularize* the multidimensionality of self. The patient's shaping role in the present in the process of *constructing* an identity is also neglected when there is a nostalgic theoretical emphasis on *discovering* an antecedent self in the past prior to traumatization.

There are several problems with the classical and developmental arrest paradigms. Such visions provide insufficient resources for the value conundrums and moral conflicts our patients confront in a world of unprecedented and unforeseeable changes, novel familial, relational, and sociocultural arrangements, and moral and epistemological complexity and ambiguity. Patients in our world encounter a different set of challenges in living than Freud's patients or even Winnicott's or Kohut's. Questions of identity, values, and choices are different in a universe of instantaneous interglobal communication, cyberrelationships, same-sex unions, virtual realities, genetic cloning, and terrorism.

Neither the grim, stoical, lucid rationality of the classical psychoanalytic vision, nor the playful, authentic, romantic Winnicottian vision are sufficient to navigate the rocky moral waters of postmodern life. Accessing Reality or the Self—as if there were a single, pristine version of either—will not help patients negotiate the diverse and sometimes conflicting subject positions or states of subjectivity and identity one confronts in a single day. Alignment with the real or earlier versions of self will also not provide guidance in opening, in a world of shifting and shrinking boundaries, to the claims of otherness while taking care of the self. An ethics of austerity or authenticity will also not necessarily guide one in handling moral conflicts in a world of extreme emotional alienation and disconnection. Nor will the classical or developmental arrest conceptions clarify the complex issue of how to respond to wanton evil or how to integrate passion and aggression into oversaturated and depleted lives.

Both visions also unwittingly rest on antiquated, objectivistic, pre-Heisenbergian assumptions about the analyst's separation and segregation from the analytic process, which obscures the analyst's co-participation in the patient's experience of moral deliberation. In other words, in assuming that the analyst stands serenely outside the process of the patient's experience of moral choice, both the classical and developmental arrest paradigms run the risk of evading the analyst's shaping role in the analytic process of moral investigation.

With its attention to the interpersonal matrix in which humans grow and develop, contemporary relational thought seems to provide promising alternatives. Questions of values may more easily arise in a postclassical, relational universe in which neutrality is more suspect, and the shaping role of the analyst is given more prominence. In ushering in issues related to values, contemporary relational psychoanalysis affords the opportunity to raise and reflect anew on questions related to ethics.

But relational reflections on morality are hindered by a major stumbling block. When it comes to questions of morality, relational thinking is sometimes not relational *enough*.[16] Relational theorists skillfully delineate the interpersonal influences on human development and the therapeutic process. But when it comes to questions about how patients live and negotiate interpersonal realities, relational theorists all-too-often tend to adopt assumptions about selves existing in isolation that are at odds with relational thinking. Psychoanalysis is, in both senses of the word, "self-centered," by which I mean that it explores self-experience with lapidary precision and the self that it theorizes—even within most relational literature—is an egocentric version that views the other as an *object*-(without its own values, ideals, needs, and desires)-for-the-self's-use, not as a *subject*. Benjamin's[17] work on mutual recognition is an exception suggesting the generalization. That psychoanalysis—even contemporary relational versions—adopts a solipsistic view of people is suggested by (1) its notion of the other as an object; (2) its failure to articulate a workable theory of intimacy, and (3) its egocentric, impoverished account of moral responsibility. Compelling accounts of morality (or intimacy) cannot develop when the other is viewed only in terms of what he or she does or does not do for the self. When a patient struggles, for example, with whether to allow his or her aging father-in-law to move in, we analysts typically ask not "What is right?" but "What does the patient want, need, or feel?" Our very question about the needs of the solitary individual predisposes us to think about isolated, unencumbered selves, not individuals inextricably involved in a network of relationships.

A psychoanalytic view of morality underwritten by an individualistic sense of self leads to a morality rooted in the neglect of the other that provides a necessary although insufficient framework for ethics. One can only have recognition of and concern for an other who is a *subject*—someone with values, interests, desires, and needs that may be different from our own.

In a recent session Harold spoke of the way he often sacrifices himself for the needs of others. He later voiced displeasure with his gardener who raised his fee without telling him. I asked Harold if/how it affected his own thinking about fee changes. He had decided to change his policy. But he then feared that he would be "cheated." "Either you get cheated or someone else does?" I asked. "In my family things are really good or bad," he informed me. "My father was successful or the meter man turned the electricity off. There was no middle ground."

If psychoanalysis is going to speak to the concerns of people in the twenty-first century who confront complex and confusing questions about how to live, then it must do more than evade the issues of values in a misguided quest to be objective, search for the Real or the Self, or espouse an egocentric vision of morality.

Psychoanalysis, in my view, does not (nor should it try to) provide a moral code or what Eastern contemplative disciplines term a "way" of life, but it is in the business of helping people explore and address how they do in fact live their lives. And it can best do this if it is reflective about the values that shape it. To know what a cure is, to know what recovery would look like, the analyst must already have a vision of what the good life is.[18] And these visions contain explicit and hidden values that illuminate and evade human possibilities. We psychoanalysts need to be alert to, and to reflect critically upon, how our tacit values impact the treatment. The value of passion, play, leisure, and idleness, for example, is neglected in the classical psychoanalytic vision, which privileges instrumental rationality, renunciation, stoicism, and self-control. Constructive facets of unintegration essential to creativity, intimacy, and spirituality are eclipsed in the development arrest model of thinkers such as Kohut, for example, when self-cohesion is valorized.[19]

I have seen Harold over a period of time in which my own theoretical orientations have evolved. My own adherence at the beginning of Harold's treatment to a more classical Freudian orientation valuing neutrality hampered my own investigation of the influence of values in the treatment. The ideal of neutrality caused me not to question values actively—especially if he did not initiate such a discussion. We did not tend to address such issues because they rarely entered the treatment. When I found the developmental-arrest model compelling, an ethics of authenticity shaped my clinical decisions. I focused on helping Harold clarify his own wishes, desires, and needs and the way this was obscured by his tendency to accommodate to the needs of others. As more overtly relational thinking shaped my thinking, I was more attentive to interpersonal facets of the treatment, but not to morality. I saw his relationships in too self-centered a way. I privileged self-development and dichotomized self and other instead of seeing them as inextricably connected. This inhibited my capacity to see the needs of others as coequal to Harold's development. This topic, and related moral considerations, were thereby eclipsed. More recently, the centrality of morality has shaped my clinical decisions. I now see it as important to integrate rather than polarize self-care and concern for the other.

Psychoanalytic considerations of values will be deepened and enriched, in my view, when thinkers from diverse theoretical perspectives delineate and critically reflect upon the hidden and explicit values that shape their theories and practices. In that spirit, I will articulate some of the values that currently influence my own consideration of issues related to values and ethics in the hope that this spurs further dialogue. As I listened to Harold struggle with questions about how to live and treat others—questions related to morality and values—I was aware of at least six main lines of influence that shaped how I responded to him: (1) an Aristotelian view of the analyst's role in the therapeutic process, (2) a pluralistic view of theory, (3) a genetic-existential view of human beings and change, (4) a spiritual view of the universe, (5) a "hermeneutics of suspicion," and (6) a pragmatic-aesthetic sensibility.

Psychoanalysts, from the perspective I am sketching, are less Platonists who reveal to their patients (hidden) blueprints for how to live based on the deep structure of Reality or the Self, than Aristotelians fostering an inquiry with the patient that cultivates "phronesis,"[20] or "prudence or practical wisdom."[21] Phronesis, or practical intelligence, practical reasoning, and "ethical know-how,"[22] is part of Aristotle's "critique of Plato's idea of the Good,"[23] namely, that morality is not a single, unitary essence, but a complex phenomenon that is context-dependent and concerned with the particular. Phronesis "does not make any appeal to ultimate foundations, eternal standards, or algorithms"[24] about the nature of Morality, Reality, the Self or anything else. It is, in Aristotle's words, "concerned with the variable . . . prudence studies particular goods."[25] Phronesis seems essential for moving through a shifting moral landscape with no fixed and pre-given guidelines for how to live. Particular moral dilemmas are not handled by looking to "pre-given determinate universals,"[26] but by the ability to "use ethical knowledge and apply it to the exigencies of . . . [a] concrete situation . . . there is no prior knowledge of the right means by which we realize the end."[27] Self-reflectiveness, attention to context rather than transcultural, ahistorical universals, a sense of the fallibility and provisionality of one's favored formulations, and the capacity for self-correction and self-transformation based on feedback are some of the characteristics of the moral praxis I am pointing toward. We need to engage in a searching scrutiny of our own values and their impact on the treatment. We also need to articulate local as opposed to universalistic theories. And finally, we need to realize that every theory, even the ones we most deeply cherish, is potentially revisable.

Levi-Strauss's[28] notion of *bricolage* provides a useful way of thinking about the analyst's role in navigating the pluralistic waters created by an Aristotelian perspective. Bricolage is a French term that has no precise equivalent in English. It is the art of doing whatever job one confronts with an assortment of tools. The bricoleur (the person who performs bricolage) is a "Jack of all trades" who uses a "heterogeneous repertoire of . . . bits and pieces"[29] to carry out a task. This individual recognizes that no single tool (school of psychoanalytic thought or practice) is likely to be useful for all patients—or even for a single patient in every situation. Operating in such a pluralistic manner affords a flexibility that is not readily available when one has a more singular focus. When one uses such a narrow approach, the insular "tool-and-method-pride" of specialization decried by Kohut,[30] in which each analytic school assumes it has the truth and shuns other ways of operating, it is as if one treats everything as a nail because all one has is a hammer. Intellectual bricolage, on the other hand, is a pluralistic way of thinking about theory in which one draws on a variety of theories and practices to respond to the theoretical and clinical exigencies one confronts. The tools the bricoleur uses depend on the task at hand.[31]

The answers to Harold's questions about how to live are, from my genetic-existential perspective, both found *and* created. The shaping role of the distant and proximate past *and* the contemporaneous present are *both* formative. Self-creating no less than self-discovery is essential to this process. Harold, like the rest of us, needs to creatively rework and integrate in the *present* his life experiences from the past into a particular and unique moral vision rather than be guided by the nature of Reality or earlier versions of himself.

"It is impossible to escape the impression," Freud begins *Civilization and Its Discontents*, "that many people commonly use false standards of measurement—that they seek power, success, and wealth for themselves and admire them in others, and that they underestimate what is of true value in life."[32] If power, success, and wealth—three of the cornerstones of what many people value in contemporary Western culture—are not what is of true value in life, then what is? Freud's important and neglected question opens the doorway to what might be termed the *spiritual* dimension.

There has been an increasing interest in spirituality among both analysts and patients in recent years as demonstrated by conferences on psychoanalysis and Buddhism and various books and articles on the relation of psychoanalysis and religion,[33] and psychoanalysis and Eastern thought.[34] The greater attention to spirituality, that sense of a larger (though not necessarily deistic) reality beyond the separate, self-contained self in which we are all embedded, offers a less self-centered perspective on values and morality and an additional point of view that might inform psychoanalytic reflections upon questions of ethics.

Because of my own long-standing interest in contemplative perspectives on the human condition, particularly Buddhist psychology, I saw Harold not solely in terms of a separate individual seeking self-fulfillment, but as one always and inevitably embedded in an interconnected web of relations. It was then harder to dichotomize individuation and altruism, personal fulfillment and his treatment of others. Believing that self and other are not polarized oppositions but interpenetrating facets of experience made it easier to explore areas that might ordinarily appear unworthy of further investigation. Then I might value authenticity and mutual recognition of the other as a person in his or her own right. A spiritual perspective helped me wonder about the place of acknowledgment of the other person, no less than individual fulfillment in Harold's life, whether excessive self-interest precluded other ways of seeing his life and his relationships with others. Harold and I could then more readily explore his impaired capacity for empathy and its impact on the quality of his life.

Several months ago Harold began a session describing how he felt alienated and unfulfilled. He wondered if there was more to life than material success (which he had). He indicated that "capitalism," along with his family of origin, were a major cause of his difficulties in living. He had become increasingly aware of the way he had defined himself and was driven by the mandate to acquire and consume. The more he "had" the better he imagined he was. He was beginning to feel that this was "empty" and he longed for a life of "greater depth and balance."

Many patients, like many analysts and people in general, define themselves and are driven by the urge to "justify their existence" (Joel Kramer, personal communication, 1998). Acquiring and consuming (money, prestige, power, goods, or substances) are two frequently traveled routes to this end. Analysts witness on a daily basis the way this breeds emptiness, deprivation, and anomie for many patients. Many analysands, like Harold, long for lives of greater meaning and substance.

From a spiritual perspective of nonduality, or oneness, Harold would be sowing the seeds of his ultimate discontent by seeing himself as separate from (and opposed to) his clients and focusing only on his own individual fulfillment. Harold and his clients, viewed nondualistically, are all in this life together, and concern with the needs of others, no less than with self-actualization, is part of living a full and meaningful life. Attachment to materialism, from a spiritual perspective, would be to "underestimate what is of true value in life" and would be an inevitable source of unhappiness and suffering. By lessening the barrier between self and others a nondualistic perspective could also foster a depthful sense of compassion for, and equanimity about, the predicaments we and our patients share—what Shakespeare termed the "ten thousand shocks that flesh is heir to." The kind of compassion I am pointing toward is deeper and more extensive than our ordinary conceptions of it—universal as opposed to local compassion. Our circle of concern embraces more of humanity than only our family and friends.

Contemplative traditions might teach psychoanalysis about the cost of neglecting spirituality; the way a purely self-centered secular orientation might breed the very egocentricity, addiction to materialism, disconnection from others, and malaise that patients may, in part, seek therapy to remedy. Psychoanalysis, since Freud, has had a tragic cast, in which renunciation and resignation, as opposed to self-realization, is the acme of mental health. A tragic vision untempered by romanticism, by a visionary hope in the possibility of transformation and improvement, is inherently resignatory and pessimistic and thereby conservative.

A third influence on my work with Harold was conceiving of psychoanalysis as what Ricoeur[35] termed a "hermeneutics of suspicion," a discipline that is interested in hidden motivations and meanings. This perspective alerted me to the way contemplative traditions no less than psychoanalysis are not without unconsciousness. Spiritual traditions simplify morality by neglecting the shaping power of unconsciousness. If spirituality can deabsolutize the self-centered psychoanalytic self, then psychoanalysis might deprovincialize the nonself-centered, spiritual self.[36] If contemplative traditions might teach psychoanalysis about the limitations of its tragic vision and its egocentric, aspiritual psychology and morality, psychoanalysis might teach spiritual traditions about the dangers of uncritical romanticism and an apsychological morality.[37] Romanticism oblivious to a tragic consciousness can be naive and ungrounded. It is more difficult, if not more self-deceptive, to take religious claims about altruism (or anything else) at face value in a post-Freudian world in which unconsciousness pervades human life and we are not even masters of our own minds.[38] Nonpsychoanalytic spiritual conceptions of morality tend to neglect the psychological complexity of ethics, the way, for example, that unconscious motives may underlie a particular conscious action or intention. Generosity, for example, may secretly fuel self-aggrandizement or self-deprivation, and self-abasement can masquerade as spiritual asceticism. Attunement to the shaping role of unconsciousness helps me explore with patients involved in contemplative traditions and practices the hidden meanings, functions, and relational configurations of their spiritual commitments. Harold and I eventually realized, for example, that attempting to live up to spiritual ideals was an unconscious method he had used to disprove his internalized conviction that he was fundamentally a bad man so that he might finally gain his father's unrequited emotional love.

A deconstructive interest in silenced or neglected perspectives emerged from my hermeneutics of suspicion. In my work with Harold, the absence of altruism as well as the presence of self-care became an area of exploration. Adopting a deconstructive perspective aids the analyst in detecting neglected and marginalized values in an analysand's life—what Foucault termed "subjugated knowledges."[39] The analyst and analysand can then more readily explore what it might mean in the latter's life if such things were valued rather than obscured.

Since there is no immaculate perception or theorizing, whatever values inform the treatment are not chosen, according to my pragmatic-aesthetic perspective, because they correspond to the way things really are, which is often complex, ambiguous, and contestable, but because they appeal to the therapist and the patient on pragmatic and aesthetic as opposed to epistemological grounds.[40] We find such values compelling and pleasing because they offer useful (not absolute) tools to address the kinds of questions we grapple with and they resonate with and point toward the sort of world we wish to inhabit and the type of life we hope to live.

A pragmatic orientation has at least six of the following elements. First, pragmatism realizes that reality is more complex than our theories. A pragmatist, like Isaiah Berlin's "foxes," distrusts Big Truths, and is interested in many things. "The fox knows many things," claims Berlin (borrowing from Archilochus), "but the hedgehog knows one big thing."[41] Pragmatism realizes that every inquiry—whether one is a hedgehog or a fox—begins with what Gadamer[42] terms prejudgments, which refer to the presuppositions that shape our apprehension and engagement with what we are encountering, whether a text or a person. One cannot put all claims in jeopardy all at once.[43] We tend to think we are more free of prejudices than our predecessors, but we too have blinders and blind spots that cannot be avoided. We cannot eliminate the presuppositions and values shaping our presence in the treatment, but they must be critically examined. Examining their shaping impact on our theorizing about morality in psychoanalytic sessions renders their influence less unconscious.

Because the map of psychoanalytic theories never completely does justice to the terrain of our patient's lives, pragmatism advocates a thoroughgoing fallibilism in which we recognize that every theory and interpretation—no matter how sacred—is open to reexamination. For example, in the course of writing this chapter, my view of pragmatism has been revised. I am now more aware of certain unresolved problems with it such as the absence of criteria for justifying its commitments. "Relativism is an excellent antidote to absolutism," notes Joel Kramer, "but you cannot build a system around it" (Joel Kramer, personal communication, 1998). Conventional standards that often inform pragmatic views of justification such as internal consistency, economy of explanation, and agreement with existing communities of discourse are themselves, as history has repeatedly shown, insufficient for justifying one's theoretical claims. The agreement of an interpretive community may, in certain cases, normalize shared blind spots and thus perpetuate regressive intellectual, social, and political assumptions, rather than shine a bright light on Truth. Witness the fact that until fairly recently the psychoanalytic literature on homosexuality has been homophobic. Positivistic science, which has been thoroughly critiqued in contemporary science, was, at one time, not a problematic perspective but a valued way of seeking truth.

Psychoanalysis needs a "critical pluralism"[44] that acknowledges the need for plurality without jettisoning the importance of decisions about quality. Postmodern discourse has usefully highlighted the false pretensions of theories that purport to be objective and universally valid. We now know with increasing clarity that there is no impartial theorizing. But postmodern discourse all too often throws out the baby of validity with the bathwater of objectivity—by which I mean that it inhibits the development of criteria for choosing a particular theory in the act of pointing out that theories are inevitably subjective and partial. Without any criteria for why one chooses a particular theory, theories become homogenized and flattened. This lacuna in postmodern discourse evades crucial questions about quality and criteria of validity that are essential for psychoanalytic treatment. Psychoanalysis, unlike much postmodern discourse, contains the resources for "metatheoretical relativism," which "denies ethical objectivism (that there is just one correct moral evaluation) without believing that all moral evaluations are equally worthy."[45] Our beliefs are, from a pragmatist perspective, provisional and endlessly contestable.

The constitutive role of contingency and chance is the fourth characteristic of a pragmatic orientation. Unpredictable elements as well as deterministic forces shape our theories and commitments. We thus need to leave room in our thinking for unsuspected possibilities. New informational technologies and developments may, for example, shape self-experience and moral decision-making in unpredictable ways.

A pragmatist realizes that there are many other ways of thinking about things. Such a person also recognizes that others usually believe in the ultimate validity of their own visions. Different perspectives are not necessarily incommensurable. While they cannot be seamlessly fused, they can sometimes be heuristically juxtaposed and even critically compared. Tolerance of, and an interest in, the value of others perspectives is crucial. The "need to nurture a critical community of inquirers"[46] is the fifth essential facet of a pragmatic orientation. Because no single perspective has a monopoly on truth, investigators need to be open to a variety of viewpoints. Critical dialogue among a diversity of viewpoints is thus crucial in the developmental of any perspective. Through such dialogue, one's own favored conceptions can be challenged and gaps or tensions in one's own perspective might be elucidated. Then, all of our moral visions can be complicated and enriched. Dialogues with colleagues in the course of writing this chapter have helped me see the Aristotelian, pragmatic, and spiritual perspectives in a different light. Let me cite two examples: one limitation of the Aristotelian framework is that it may neglect the value of imprudence. Morality (and health) may involve, in certain circumstances, excess and rebellion, not moderation and judiciousness. "The road of excess leads to the palace of wisdom," Blake reminds us.[47] The immoderate tactics of Christ,

Gandhi, and Martin Luther King Jr., for example, have enriched human wel-fare. Second, in valorizing oneness and selflessness, spiritual perspectives on real-ity, may neglect the dizzying diversity of the world and the dangers of a self-sacrificing, renunciate morality. Spiritual traditions can provide moral visions and values but not fully elaborated analytical tools to explore and understand immorality. The details of a spiritually attuned hermeneutics of sus-picion also need further delineation and elaboration.

All moral visions have personal and social consequences. A pragmatist believes that all of these are not equally worthy. While there are many human goods—ranging from a self-centered focus on self-realization to an other-regarding emphasis of spiritual worldviews on cultivating selflessness, compas-sion, and love for others—not all are equally good. The moral universe of a Shakespearian tragedy is more complex, compelling, and edifying than the flat-tened world of a fundamentalist cult or a soap opera. Part of the critical dia-logue among a variety of perspectives that pragmatism recommends thus involves consideration of the differing consequences of particular moral per-spectives. For example: What is the impact on the treatment and the patient when an individualistic ethos with self-enhancement and personal achievement as the highest good underlies the analyst's moral stance? On the other hand, how is the patient affected when the analyst believes in a more communitarian philosophy that assumes certain perils to individualism and values relatedness and connectedness?[48] What kinds of worlds are created when either vision pre-dominates in one's life?

The topic of psychoanalysis and morality, from the perspective that I have been presenting in this chapter, refers to at least two different things: the uncon-scious moralities and value systems implicit in our psychoanalytic theories and practices and how to deal with particular moral conflicts (reporting on cheat-ing, contact with a deadbeat Dad, having an abortion, and so forth). Up till now in this chapter I have focused on the first topic. Before concluding, I will explore briefly the second.

Moral philosophers, according to Jones, have distinguished two different approaches to understanding moral decision making: a "deontological" approach in which ethics entails developing a "calculus of moral reasoning and refining and applying moral principles" and an "ethics of character," involving becoming a certain sort of person.[49] There are several ways that psychoanalysis can contribute to the second type of moral decision making. Psychoanalysis cannot offer a fixed moral calculus, but with its attention to the developmental nature of moral beliefs, the ubiquity of unconsciousness, and our inevitable embeddedness in various relational matrixes, psychoanalytic treatment does provide a unique atmosphere to explore moral conflicts, and aid individuals in detecting moral self-blindness and cultivating greater ethical sensitivity to other people. From this third, relational perspective, the analyst is a kind of Aris-totelian engaged in a self-reflexive dialogue with the analysand about the

developmental origins of his or her morality and the contemporaneous consequences for self and other of one's moral beliefs and actions, rather than a Platonist aiding the patient in getting in touch with Reality or the Self. Becoming
moral, from this perspective, involves cultivating greater relational sensitivity
and attunement, moral know-how, and self-understanding in the patient.

Morality, like all facets of psychological life, is partially, although not completely, unconscious. Freud was not the first person to consider unconsciousness
in the moral domain. Spinoza and Dewey, among many others, also recognized
it.[50] But psychoanalytic treatment explores and reveals the unconscious ideals
and values that undergird and are often opaque to ordinary introspection or
even meditative contemplation. Psychoanalysis can, for example, pinpoint and
reveal the costs of hidden aims, desires, and fears that shape our values. Let me
give an example. A deep Calvinist streak permeates Western civilization. There
is what Fromm[51] terms a taboo on selfishness in modern culture. From this perspective, to be self-centered is to be sinful and to be selfless is to be virtuous.[52]
Conquering selfishness is one important purpose of spiritual ethics. It is
assumed by many contemplative traditions that when human beings are left to
their own devices they will be destructively egocentric, even evil. Psychoanalysis deconstructs the self-betraying, even self-neglectful, propensities of renun-
ciative spiritual viewpoints as well as the self-aggrandizing tendencies endemic
to egocentric secular values. Each is an inadequate foundation for living a more
moral life. When virtue entails renunciation of our humanness (e.g., our self-
centeredness and our carnality), as in much contemplative thought, then self-
care is deeply compromised. When self-inflation is the highest virtue, as in
much secular thought, one falls prey to an alienating egocentricity, which precludes altruism and connectedness to others. Recognition of the other is then
deeply neglected.

The dualist subject–object split underlying Western thought—particularly
science and philosophy—undermines reflections on morality. It causes us to
think of ourselves as self-encapsulated monads. Such a perspective is a problematic basis for contemplating ethics for it inevitably polarizes the claims of
the other and the needs of the self. Self-care and altruism are then erroneously
treated as opposed rather than mutually interpenetrating. Psychoanalysis offers
the potential of a more nondualistic, relational perspective about morality. In
revealing the irreducible interconnectedness of human beings, contemporary
relational psychoanalysts—whether object relational, self psychological, neo-
Freudian, interpersonal, or intersubjective—open up the potential of conceiving of the other as a subject with his or her own unique values and needs, not
an object-for-the-self's-use. An implicit (and perhaps not yet fully mined)
implication of these disparate perspectives is that morality is a property of a
relation between differently constituted persons, not a possession of an isolated
mind. A morality involving what Benjamin[53] terms "mutual recognition" of the
claims of self and other could thereby be fostered.

There are a plurality of ends that might be pursued in a particular treatment ranging from the rationality and stoicism valued by Freud to the authenticity and aliveness cherished by Winnicott. The psychoanalyst's role in a treatment that was attuned to the moral domain cannot be exhaustively delineated. Much depends on the particular therapeutic context, including the unique nature and needs of the analysand. Clarifying the analysand's existing values, pinpointing the developmental origins and contemporary meanings and functions of those values, and cultivating ethical attentiveness and know-how may all be operative in different ways at different times. The analyst's role is protean, depending on the needs of a particular patient, which will obviously differ in each case. With a patient such as Harold, the analyst might question or even challenge his moral code by asking unsettling questions about gaps or inconsistencies or tensions. The analyst might actively question the psychological impact of following the moral code that the patient has unquestioningly inherited from her parents and/or the culture in which she lives. The analyst might also question the analysand's taken-for-granted narrative about himself and his moral relation to others and the world. The shaping influence of the analyst's active stance regarding the patient's relation to morality would, of course, need to be explored and understood. More inclusive moral perspectives about the patient's life might develop. Harold, for example, acquired more of a sense of concern for others in the course of treatment. He became more capable of balancing altruism and self-care.

In other cases the analyst may assist the patient in challenging self-nullifying familial values or oppressive cultural ambitions and ideals. With a disillusioned, but highly successful lawyer who felt unfulfilled and deprived in the adversarial world of his profession, I questioned the stifling materialistic values he had internalized from his father that defined him only in terms of how hard he worked, how much he earned, and how much he owned. As I raised questions about his image of male success, we learned that he felt like a disappointment to his critical and high-achieving parents and endeavored to *justify* his existence through professional success and personal acquisitions. As we began to understand the way achievements and products were an attempt to replace his emotional hunger and deprivation, he initiated a critical examination of the values that had fueled his one-dimensional pursuit of power and money. He began to feel that other ways of living might be possible. He eventually cut back his hours at work, reduced his compulsive conspicuous consumption, became more involved in raising his children, and took more time for sunsets, family picnics, and relationships with friends.

For a depressed, divorced woman from a patriarchal foreign culture who had been abused in her arranged marriage, the treatment questioned her belief in her second-class status and validated her inchoate sense that she was entitled to a relationship of equality with a man. As I supported her challenging of culturally sanctioned values that she had internalized about women's inferior status in relation to men, her depression began to lift and she sought equitable treatment from her partners.

With another person the analyst coparticipates in the creation, rather than the deconstruction, of a moral code. Here one facilitates the patient's development of moral values and the capacity for moral reasoning. Clarifying existing moral ideals, delineating the developmental origins and contemporary meanings and functions of the analysand's values, or refining the patient's ethical "phronesis" or know-how play a less central role, at least for a time. With a passive and detached young woman from an emotionally neglectful home, who felt that she was not entitled to a life—let alone a choice about her own values—the treatment provided a context in which she could engage in a noncoercive dialogue about her values, ideals, desires, and needs. She had been profoundly silenced by her highly competent and self-preoccupied parents. As we explored this theme as it became enacted within the therapeutic relationship, particularly the way she tried to accommodate to what she thought I wanted, she gradually began to acknowledge and integrate what had been denied and buried in her family. As the grip of her lifelong self-nullification was broken, she developed more self-trust in her own moral vision. She was eventually able to create a moral code based on her values rather than automatic and unconscious submission and accommodation to others. She also developed greater empathy for the pain of other women who had been victimized.

Here are some of the questions psychoanalysts might ask in a psychoanalysis that was open to the moral domain: What are the hidden moralities shaping the analyst's participation in analysis? Does the analyst or the patient avoid any moral issues? What are the multiple meanings, origins, psychological functions, and relational consequences of the moralities the patient and the analyst believe in? What are the costs of each? How does the analyst's moral stance affect treatment? How do we develop a relational morality? What is the impact of cultural context(s) and constraints on psychoanalytic reflections on morality? What are the moral costs of the "new capitalism," in which job security is more tenuous, careers are shorter-lived, workers are eminently disposable, and vocational trust and loyalty toward work have eroded? What new moral dilemmas are raised by communication technologies such as e-mail, virtual realities, and so forth? What moral implications do synthetic forms of life ranging from virtual realities to "prosthetic" technologies such as breast enlargement surgery for cosmetic reasons have for analysts and patients? What moral conundrums are stirred up by nontraditional forms of family life/structure—such as same-sex unions, single parent homes, and families in which both parents are away working for extensive periods of time?

Whatever our task in specific cases, psychoanalytic reflections on values and ethics will be invigorated and enriched when psychoanalysts and interested thinkers from allied fields make explicit and reflect upon the variety of values informing their stance toward treatment. I have tried to point out gaps and raise questions about several dominant psychoanalytic stances toward living a moral life. I have also articulated some of the values shaping my own consideration of ethics in treatment, as well as the partiality of my own perspective, in the hope that it will spur further dialogue on this important and neglected topic. Aware of the importance of the task and the incompleteness of my own vision, I take solace in a remark by Rabbi Tarphon in *Pirke Aboth: The Ethics of the Fathers.* "The work is not yours to finish; but neither are you free to take no part in it."[54]

CHAPTER THREE

Psychoanalysis at Play in the Garden of Love

Although a strong egoism is a protection against falling ill, in the last resort we must begin to love others in order not to fall ill.

—Sigmund Freud

We coupled, so sane and insane.
—Ann Sexton

SHAKESPEARE WAS ENCHANTED BY IT. Beckett was skeptical of it. Freud knew that without it we will fall ill. It is at once erotic and sublime, terrifying and entrancing, transformative and destabilizing. It is something that most people (except a monk, a nun, or a hermit) seek but tend to lose, feeling buoyed and sustained when it is present and deprived and bereft when it is absent. What is this mesmerizing and unsettling phenomena we call love? Love has altered history, generated great works of art, instigated infamous crimes of passion, fueled national disasters, consoled the downtrodden, and ennobled us all. It creates our greatest pain and our most momentous awakenings.

Love is arguably the most frequent theme in popular culture. But the "love" presented in soap operas, romance novels, popular songs, and the lives of celebrities often is a degraded and impoverished version,[1] beset by empty images and illusions. The version of love portrayed in popular culture is usually completely unrealistic or unrequited, unsubstantial or illusory. Love is depicted in television and in films as an instantaneous and effortless communion and bliss

45

or an impossibility because of the human predilection for infidelity and betrayal. Happily ever after is what almost every Hollywood movie implies. Movies end when the relationship begins. *Sleepless in Seattle*, like the vast majority of Hollywood films, focuses all its attention on the yearning to be connected, not the actual relationship. The whole movie is about the prelude and the first hour of the relationship between Tom Hanks and Meg Ryan. We never see what happens after they meet—just as we never saw Ozzie and Harriet fight.

In films that purport to present a more realistic conception of intimacy and love, like *Your Friends and Neighbors*, there is little friendship and less love. But there is plenty of nonstop emotional and sexual infidelity and betrayal. The lives of politicians and religious leaders, like the hyperbolic and jaded world of popular culture, herald the insubstantiality and ultimate illusoriness of love.

The desecration of love in our culture is tragic, given the state of the world. We live in an time characterized by profound alienation, disconnection, and anomie. There are pervasive assaults on our privacy, dignity, and freedom. This occurs in a secular sociohistorical context in which humans are disconnected from larger traditional religious frameworks of understanding and solace, which provide ultimate direction and meaning. The freedom of the individual ushered in by modernism, with its questioning of the person's role in a larger cosmos informed by a religious view of the universe, was purchased at the cost of disconnecting humans from larger, transhuman sources of meaning. In other words, humans came to live their own lives even as they were cast adrift, devoid of comfort-generating larger frameworks of beliefs that lent life significance. Without ultimate meaning or direction, humans are thrown back on narrowed and flattened lives of self-absorption, accountable only to the dictates of their individual conscience.[2] Such a secular view of the world fosters egocentricity and hedonism and ultimately creates an emptiness in people's lives.

Humans need transcendence, values beyond the isolated, encapsulated self and its well-being and survival. But there is no transcendence in our age: The old gods—religion, the Communist Party, the proletariat, psychoanalysis—compel less enthusiasm. This absence of viable ideals generates a haunting void. Love provides a "lateral" rather than a "vertical" transcendence, by which I mean that ultimate value is in the loving connection with another person outside ourselves rather than in our devotion to a "higher" cause or an external ideology whether religious, psychological, or political.[3] Love allows us to surmount our self-encapsulation, isolation, and egoism and find meaning and worth beyond ourselves.

Love has an ambivalent status in psychoanalysis. On the one hand, "to love and to work," *liebe* and *arbeit,* were, according to Freud, a sign of mental health.[4] The crucial importance that loving and being loved play in the happiness and fulfillment of the lives of those we work with is evident to all psychoanalysts.[5] The capacity to love makes a person truly human. And yet, despite love's extraordinary importance in the lives of individuals, it has been a curiously neglected topic in the psychoanalytic literature. To be sure, to love and to work have served, since Freud, as an implicit touchstone for mental health in the clinical work of many psychoanalysts. But what is love or "lieben"? And what fuels and what diminishes it? Ever since Freud's *Three Essays on the Theory of Sexuality*, psychoanalysts have evinced interest in sexuality and its vicissitudes. But the psychoanalytic literature is ironically lacking in direct discussions of the love that Freud acknowledged as central to human life. When psychoanalysts have written about romantic love[6] they have generally focused more on the "vicissitudes of falling in love than how it is sustained."[7] Psychoanalysts have thus illuminated more about what erodes intimacy than what fosters it.

And yet, despite the paucity of data on love in the psychoanalytic literature, psychoanalysis has the potential to illuminate its many dimensions, including what nurtures it. The sanctuary of the analytic encounter and the emphasis on human subjectivity, relatedness, and intimacy—in their myriad conscious and unconscious expressions—provides a unique environment to reflect on what nourishes and what distorts and complicates love. Analysts hear, on a daily basis, about love lost and found, consummated and abated. Surely, this could be a unique laboratory in which to study love.

It could be argued that to theorize about love is to violate its ineffable spirit and reduce its complexity. "Our meddling intellect," notes Wordsworth, "mis-shapes the beauteous forms of things;/-We murder to dissect."[8] Certainly there is a danger in theoretically reflecting on love—namely, that we can intellectualize about it and thus reduce or distort it. But articulating what interferes with and what fosters love can also have salutary consequences.

Love is an enormously complex phenomena composed of many facets that obviously can be approached from many angles, including the historical, psychological, social, sexual, and religious. There are many kinds of love: the love of the religious seeker for the divine, the mystic for the cosmos, the philosopher for wisdom, the citizen for her community, the artist for beauty, the parent, for her child or the child for his parent, and the lover for his or her partner.

In this chapter I focus on those psychological forces that foster and nourish a loving interpersonal relationship between two adults rather than on these other kinds of love or those psychological forces that erode love in a relationship.[9] I will have accomplished my purpose if we all return to what we love—whether our spouse, nature, a child, the divine, even psychoanalysis—with renewed curiosity, appreciation, and passion.

In the first section I explore the fate of love in psychoanalytic discourse, particularly why love has been resisted in psychoanalysis. I highlight several reasons, including Jung's break from Freud, the tragic psychology of psychoanalysis, psychoanalysis's hermeneutics of suspicion, and psychoanalysis's egocentric vision of selfhood.[10] Then I examine some of the psychodynamic factors that erode love.[11] In the conclusion I offer recommendations for opening up pathways to love and sustaining it. Chief among them is the creation of a romantic space, that is, an atmosphere in the relationship in which there is openness, playfulness, an acceptance of multiple perspectives on reality and each other. A harmonious integration of many seemingly oppositional but mutually enriching qualities such as security and risk/exploration, passion and reflectiveness, autonomy and intimacy, power and surrender, and a capacity to relate to each other in richly varied ways are also crucial.

Psychoanalysis has had more to say about the pathology of love relations than its constructive dimensions. There may be at least five reasons for the dearth of analytic literature on this topic and the lacuna within psychoanalysis.

Clinical data on love are difficult to obtain because one is less likely to initiate treatment when in love than when one's heart has been broken. And patients who are in treatment speak more frequently of love's absence rather than its presence. Analysts then hear, in the consulting room, about love lost and unrequited, not consummated. Second, psychoanalysis, as I have suggested earlier, is underwritten by a "tragic" view of the universe,[12] highlighting the inescapable irrationality, illusions, and conflict that permeate human experience, including love. When analysts listen to reports of love, they often question the conscious motives and meanings of the speaker, assuming that what is at stake is more complex and elusive than the person knows.[13] This perspective is tremendously useful in revealing hidden facets of what we ordinarily evade. Without concerted effort, these dimensions of ourselves, such as our fear and shame, envy and aggression, remain disavowed and concealed, exerting a powerful and destructive influence on our relationships and the quality of our lives. But the hermeneutics of suspicion has its own hidden implications, no less formative for being unconscious. Psychoanalysis deconstructs 'positive' experiences such as love—looking for its illusions, empty idealizations, and its seamy underside—but rarely explores whether afflictive emotions such as hate or jealousy are ever a protection against love.[14] Humanly enriching experiences such as love or spirituality are assumed a priori to be illusions or delusions while 'negative' emotions such as hostility or envy are assumed to be realistic, just the ways things are. Assuming that afflictive emotions are the fundamental human reality makes it nearly impossible to ask what they might be disavowing.

One source of interpretive error, according to Freud, as I mentioned earlier, is "the Charybdis of judging the normal entirely by the standards of the pathological."[15] Psychoanalysts are all too often reductionistic in thinking about love relations, often approaching patients' accounts of love by falling victim to a priori pathologizing. The ears of psychoanalysts are then tuned toward the disavowed and the problematic facets of love, its illusions and denials, not its life-enhancing and transforming dimensions. Thus the emphasis is more on the delusions than the possibilities of love, with psychoanalysts viewing love in too grim a light. "Mature love in much of the analytic literature," notes Mitchell, "often seems a somber, dispassionate affair, indistinguishable from mourning."[16]

The third reason that love may be neglected in psychoanalysis is that it is, as I suggested in chapter two, inherently self-centered: discovering and strengthening the self is the central focus of psychoanalytic treatment, with the self that it strengthens an egocentric version that views the other not as a separate subject with its own unique wishes, goals, values, and needs, but in terms of what it does (or does not) provide for the self. Psychoanalysts have distinguished between healthy and pathological narcissism. Even in the case of the former, an unconscious egocentricity is operative. While the relational revolution in contemporary analysis has highlighted the intersubjective nature of human development and the psychoanalytic process, psychoanalysis has historically neglected the subjectivity of the extraanalytic other (e.g., the patient's parents, spouse, or lover), which has impeded our capacity to conceive of that other as an equal subject not simply as an object-for-the-subject's-use. Benjamin points psychoanalysis in exactly the direction it needs to go when she writes "where objects were, subjects must be."[17] It is not accidental that psychoanalysis does not have a workable theory of intimacy. For intimacy cannot thrive in a world in which the other is viewed only as an object or thing that did (or did not) fulfill the needs of the self.[18]

The split between Freud and some of his followers such as Jung, who explored love from a less pathological perspective, has marginalized Jungian thought and segregated it from mainsteam psychoanalysis. Jung examined some of the ingredients of love, including the integration of male and female characteristics, which he termed *anima* and *animus*. He felt that men needed to connect with and cultivate their feminine side, while women needed to experience and develop their masculine side. Psychoanalysis was deprived of Jung's prospective focus, and his more progressivistic accounts of love (and spirituality). This is the fourth factor causing psychoanalysis to give short shrift to love.

And finally, jealousy of our patients' accounts of love may sometimes unconsciously predispose psychoanalysts to reduce rather than appreciate their discussions about it. Some analysts may have difficulty acknowledging the existence of a wondrous experience that they themselves may be lacking. I wonder if many analysts may not pay attention to the transforming aspects of love relationships outside the analytic situation because they need to see transformation as related primarily (if not solely) to the analytic relationship.

For all these reasons, and probably others that I have not recognized, psychoanalysts may be looking for love in all the wrong places and so have a skewed view of it. It is no wonder that some patients fear that therapists are, in Yalom's felicitous phrase, "love's executioners."[19]

As a springboard to consider love and it vicissitudes, consider the song "Unforgettable You," which in several short verses to a beautiful melody, speaks

of a completely captivating and entrancing love: "That someone so unforgettable / Thinks that I am unforgettable, too."

The second vignette describes a marriage:

> you live in the everyday again, which is truth, with pyjamas and a
> toothbrush in your foamy mouth in front of the other, with classical
> nakedness in the bath that does not excite . . . the other's early life is a
> book you think you know as you know a classic, a bit dusty already. . . .
> The past is no secret any longer, the present is thin because it is worn
> out day by day, and the future means growing old.[20]

Many relationships begin with the enthrallment, idealization, and passion
depicted in Nat King Cole's classic song, "Unforgettable," and succumb to the
familiarity and banality, disappointment and deprivation of the prosaic marriage
in Max Frisch's *Gantenbein* in the second. These vignettes, like patients' troubled
and poignant accounts of love and its vicissitudes (love that is consummated and
eventually eroded, unrequited or betrayed), raise several questions of central
concern for psychoanalysts. Why is enduring love that integrates passion and
emotional trust, mutual respect and commitment so elusive? Why does love so
frequently erode over time? How might a couple create a romantic space in
which love flourishes?

Every school of psychoanalysis contributes to an understanding of what
interferes with and what fosters love. From classical psychoanalysis we become
more attuned to the transferential aspects of love, by which I mean the way pro-
totypes of our adult loves are taken from childhood figures. "Love," notes Freud,
"consists of new editions of old traits and . . . it repeats infantile reactions."[21]
The past, in this view, may not simply be prologue but a straitjacket, causing us
to emotionally gravitate toward people who resemble important figures from
our past even if we have had an emotionally difficult and unsatisfying relationship with them. We then relate to lovers in the present in similar and restrictive
ways. Freud goes on to say that the love that "appears in ordinary life and is
called normal," in contrast to transference love, the situational love for the analyst, is less dependent on the infantile pattern and more adaptable and capable
of modification.[22]

Classical analysis also alerts us to the importance of resolving oedipal conflicts and integrating passion and tenderness. Unresolved oedipal conflicts lead
to guilt and sexual inhibitions that obviously hinder the development of a
loving relationship. Describing a condition he termed "psychical impotence,"
Freud aptly noted the pervasive difficulty most people have integrating tender
and passionate feelings. Such people, according to Freud, rarely feel physically
passionate about those people who they feel emotional tenderness toward.[23]
Many analysands hunger for those people who are emotionally unavailable and
devalue those who are. Clinicians witness this dynamic frequently, hearing
reports about partners of patients who are intelligent and kind but "boring" or

"unexciting." Or we get reports about people who are sexually stimulating but emotionally distant and detached. In patients for whom tension, strife, or even degradation were a prelude to parental contact or love, meaningful relationships in the present without difficulty or discord feel strange, unfamiliar, and empty. Such patients often devalue people who treat them well and seek people who are emotionally unavailable. They are intrigued by partners who keep them dangling on a string, and inevitably feel that something is "missing" with mates who are responsive to them.

Drawing on classical psychoanalysis and object relations theory Kernberg[24] has pointed out additional psychodynamic obstacles to intimacy ranging from the absence of positive preoedipal experiences with sensuous body care to failure to resolve oedipal conflicts. Kernberg notes that some people do not have the capacity to relate to others as whole people with diverse and sometimes conflicting qualities. Such people cannot integrate positive and negative feelings about others (e.g., warmth and aggression) into a single image of them. Disturbing qualities such as resentment or even hate cannot be reconciled with affection and tenderness; anger or jealousy threaten to overwhelm affectionate feelings. Or emotional love cannot be integrated with one's physical passion.

Kernberg[25] pinpoints another obstacle to love. For certain individuals, those who lack a sense of identity and have difficulty maintaining stable boundaries between self and other, emotional and physical intimacy is total and destabilizing or nonexistent. There is either no relationship or a complete and terrifying fusion or merger.

From Winnicott and British middle school object relations theory, analysts have become more aware of how many individuals have been profoundly impinged upon by unattuned caregivers in infancy and childhood and have developed a compensatory overlay, a false self accommodation that keeps the authentic self hidden so that it is not violated or squashed. Such people have great difficulty bringing themselves into relationships because they are endangered by intimacy. For people who have been deeply intruded upon by emotionally starved parents throughout their lives, intimacy—which entails opening up one's boundaries—means surrendering to the self-centered need of the other, which triggers the deadly possibility that one will lose oneself.

The Fairbairnian wing of object relations theory also has alerted us to the way love is endangered by repetitive and restrictive internalized object relations or views of and relationships between self and other. Fairbairn pinpointed the way we habitually repeat old internalized interpersonal scenarios in the present in relationships, some of which hinder intimacy. These relational patterns shaped by past interactions with caregivers or significant people in our lives such as siblings can take many forms. Fairbairn highlights our tendency to blame ourselves and hold ourselves completely responsible for interpersonal conflicts while taking the other person "off the hook." It is "better to be a sinner in a world ruled by God," notes Fairbairn, "than to live in a world ruled by the devil."[26] In other words, we blame ourselves (we are the sinner) and then convince ourselves that the universe is ordered and just, our parents (and our spouse) are reasonable, and we feel protected and safe. In one stroke we thus explain away the deprivation and suffering of the past and desperately keep alive the hope that we may finally receive in the present the love and connectedness that was not forthcoming from caregivers in the past. This is one reason many people tolerate abuse or deprivation or lovelessness in their relationships.

Self psychology alerts us to the obstacles to love generated by self-vulnerability. Since the advent of self psychology, psychoanalytic clinicians are more attuned to the strategies that fragile, terrified, or besieged selves utilize to buttress and fortify themselves, ranging from expecting perfect attunement from their spouse to seeking connections with powerful others who are enlisted to protect and sustain them. In certain patients with such vulnerability, for example, intimacy is not sought simply for its own sake but to heal or strengthen the self. Experiencing themselves as weak and bereft, these individuals, what Bach terms "deflated narcissists," seek ideal or powerful partners in order to complete them.[27] One form this takes for some women is to seek relationships with powerful men who offer the promise of protecting them, in order to allay deep-seated feelings of inferiority and insecurity. Another form is illustrated by those men who seek a woman who is a mother figure who will keep their lives running smoothly, rather than a partner for a mutually gratifying adult intimacy.

In illuminating the vicissitudes of narcissism, Kohut and his collaborators and successors elucidated another barrier to love. Mutuality is essential to love, as Benjamin has noted from a contemporary object relations perspective.[28] Dominance or submission compromises the mutual recognition between two people treated as equals that is essential for intimacy. Healthy intimacy occurs when there is a mutually respectful and empowering relation between two people. Intimacy, according to Benjamin, necessitates that couples integrate mutual recognition as well as self-assertion and individuation. Narcissism is antithetical to reciprocal respect. Relating to others in terms of what the person does or does not offer the self inhibits mutuality. Extreme self-investment can render the other person invisible. What Bach calls "overinflated narcissists," on the other hand, who experience themselves as the center of the universe, denigrate the very partners whose love they need.[29] Love does not live when we conceive of the other narcissistically, in terms only of what he or she can do for the self, rather than what the self might do for the other. This takes the form of expecting one's spouse to provide "perfect mirroring," to completely understand and fulfill one's needs—and to do this without one having to tell one's spouse what one desires or values.

Many people experience how passion fades over time. Ordinarily we assume that idealizations crumble under the pressure of reality and familiarity lessens newness and fosters boredom. Drawing on the sensitivity within interpersonal psychoanalysis to the search for security and the tendency for what Harry Stack Sullivan termed "selective [in]attention," Mitchell[30] has illuminated the way couples often collude in constructing an illusory security and familiarity that masks the ways in which spouses are actually complex and opaque to one another. This constructed security (rather than familiarity) dulls the relationship, leading spouses to look outside their primary relationship for adventure and passion.

Our brief survey has, I hope, alerted us to various pitfalls along the path of love. Ideally, it has also pointed toward some of the key ingredients of love, such as integrating passion with aggression, creating a new and vital relationship, and connecting with a person who unconsciously resonates with emotionally important figures from our past. It also has alerted us to the importance of attending to the needs of the other as well as the care of the self, and risking intimacy as well as constructing security.

Love resists singular definition or description. In Plato's *Symposium*, a multidimensional exploration of love in its myriad complexity, there is no final word about it. No single speech offered *the truth about love*.[31] This should give us pause.

Here is one way of thinking about love. It is always kind and patient, filled with truth and loyalty. It is devoid of envy and dissembling and is immune to erosion or decay. The following is a picture of love that often appears in religious and spiritual texts such as the first letter of St. Paul to the Corinthians, where he says in the King James version:

> Love suffereth long, and is kind; love envieth not;
> love vaunteth not itself; is not puffed up,
> Doth not behave itself unseemly; seeketh not her own,
> is not easily provoked, thinketh no evil;
> Rejoiceth not in iniquity, but rejoiceth in the truth;
> Beareth all things, believeth all things, hopeth all things,
> endureth all things.
> Love never faileth . . .
> For we know in part, and we prophesy in part.
> . . .we see through a glass, darkly; but then face to face.[32]

I'm sure many of us resonate with the inspiring words of St. Paul, who presents love as kind, ever-patient, without envy or self-conceit, devoid of unseemly behavior, never self-centered, and without evil. It endures all things and is never failing. Love is viewed as constant, unalterable, and unshakeable. It is unconditional, unbreakable, and permanent.

Paul's vision substantiates the picture many of us have of love, the version that we have been deeply socialized to hold—the image that years of television, movies, and popular songs affirm—that there is one true love, that it happens immediately, that it is destiny, a perfect union, totally secure and ever-lasting, and that it is filled with passion, honesty, loyalty, selflessness, compassion, patience, security, and unity.

But is this exalted vision true? Let's examine Paul's remarks more closely. Paul says that he "sees through a glass, darkly." He also admits that what he says "we know in part," and "we prophesy in part." Paul acknowledges that he is looking through an imperfect mirror and in part forecasting the future. We know that even a perfect mirror does not reflect perfectly; rather, it distorts. And there is no 20/20 vision when we dream about the future. Mirrors, as the artist Jean Cocteau once noted, should do a little reflecting before throwing back the image. The fact that Paul's vision is imperfect and that he speculates about the future—about what-is-not-yet—opens up the possibility that his claims are not totally binding, that he might not tell the whole story, that we might speculate anew on his conclusions and the nature of love. While he presents a deeply inspiring vision of love, it does not jibe completely with our experience, where risk sometimes upsets security, where hate cohabits with love. The experience of divorcees, as well as those of many married couples, suggest that love is not always indestructible, that it is not the solid, unshakeable, stable beacon we idealistically assume it is, but rather, it is fragile and can erode. If Paul, like us, "sees through a glass darkly," might love harbor ambivalence? Might it not always be kind? Might it sometimes generate envy? Might it lead once in a while to unseemly behavior? Might it periodically involve dissembling? Might it sometimes even fail?

Here is another way of thinking about love. We choose partners who psychologically resemble our parents. We relate to them in old, familiar, and restrictive ways. The relationship contains all the indecorous qualities that constrain the rest of our relationships. A few years ago I quipped to a friend, a student of Zen, that if one wanted to know what a Zen master was really like, then one should speak to her husband or his wife. Relationships bring out the *worst* in us as well as the best in us. What appears as love can mask hate and what seems to sustain a couple may covertly restrict them. This sobering picture of love often appears in psychological texts from Freud to the present.

The problem with apsychological spiritual accounts, such as Paul's letter to the Corinthians, is that they present an idealized and romanticized vision of love, a picture that clashes with our experience in relationships, where there is staleness as well as passion, where jealousy may sometimes coexist with idealization, where love sometimes erodes and fades. Psychoanalysis has traditionally been highly skilled at illuminating the hidden and disavowed facets of love: the way love is not always kind, the way that it may sometimes generate the worst in us and even miscarry. Psychoanalysis does us a great service by presenting a more realistic account of love that confronts rather than evades its idealizations and illusions.

The problem with psychoanalytic accounts of love is that they are too often grim and solemn, devoid of the joy and intimacy that love engenders.

Spiritual perspectives hold out the hope that there are possibilities for a love more intimate and ecstatic than psychoanalytic accounts usually describe.

Love, to borrow Pascal's description of human beings, is characterized by grandeur as well as by misery (*misère*),[33] greatness as well as wretchedness.[34] Only a view that embraces both (as well as other apparent oppositions) can illuminate love. New vistas on the nature of love might open if psychoanalysis offered a critique that was affirmative and reconstructive, not simply deconstructive and reductionistic. Psychoanalysis and love might have a better marriage if psychoanalysis drew on its fertile resources—its capacity to illuminate hidden meanings and obstacles—without forsaking the optimistic possibilities for love depicted in spiritual traditions.

W. H. Auden's homage to William Butler Yeats, "In Memory of W. B. Yeats," may give you a feeling of the elusive sensibility that I am pointing toward when he writes: "Still persuade us to rejoice/ . . . Sing of human unsuccess/In a rapture of distress/ . . . In the prison of his days/Teach the free man how to praise."[35] When psychoanalysts can aid patients in nurturing practices of love that do not simply deconstruct its illusions, then psychoanalysts might be midwives to love rather than executioners.

In conclusion, let me offer one such perspective on what nourishes love. I believe that great variations exist in the path that people travel in order to love. Historical studies of love suggest that it is protean, taking on different forms and coloration in different cultures and different ages. The qualities that I suggest are essential to a flourishing, loving relationship are, of course, shaped by my experiences, values, outlook, desires, gender, race, blind spots, and ideals. Mutual respect, sexual passion, shared values, the ability to listen and communicate, idealization, the tolerance of imperfections, humor, acceptance of differences, and the capacity to forgive are crucial for a loving relationship. So is an environment of attunement in which one feels deeply known and cherished, emotionally and physically excited, passionately connected, and enriched and enhanced. Such an atmosphere is something cocreated by both members of a relationship that must be continually nourished.

But a singular emphasis on these essential qualities or experiences neglects another crucial facet to sustaining love—namely, the creation of what Wilkinson and Gabbard term the experience of a "romantic space" in a relationship.[36] They define a romantic space as "both an intrapsychic and an interpersonal experience that sustains a feeling of being in love."[37] The notion of romantic space derives from Winnicott's concept of *potential space*. A Winnicottian potential space is a "good-enough," imaginatively generative, facilitative environment characterized by openness, playfulness, flexibility, and the capacity to perceive experience and relate to other people in a multitude of ways.[38] When a relationship is a potential space, there is the emotional safety and encouragement to relate creatively and multidimensionally so as to expand the couple's personal and relational repertoire.

Potential space: A husband places two sculpted branches he found while walking in the woods in an empty vase that his wife has put near the fireplace in their living room. The wife notices it and feels that the ad hoc "Zen sculpture" her husband had spontaneously fashioned enhances the ambience in the living room. Later in the day she finds another branch outside and adds it to the two sparse branches. The husband notices her addition, which they both feel improves the room even further. The "aesthetic jazz" that they created was synergistic—that is, it enriched both their mini-creations and their relationship.

Potential space in a relationship is an open, playful attitude and way of relating in which experimentation, inventiveness, creativity, complexity, mutual learning and growth flourish. There is a relishing of metaphor and an acceptance of multiple perspectives on reality and the relationship. Internal psychic space is expanded and the repertoire of interpersonal possibilities is increased.

Let me illustrate two of these topics—relating to one's spouse on multiple levels and in a multitude of ways, and integrating opposite qualities such as security and risk and passion and reflectiveness.

One's partner may be, at different times, many things: one's own best friend, one's lover, the mother-of-one's-child/ father-of-one's-child, a nurturing maternal presence or a protective paternal one, someone else's best friend, a cherished co-worker. When there is potential space in a relationship, one sees one's partner in a variety of ways and none is privileged or crowds out the existence of others. The variety of modes of relatedness are not collapsed into a single, flattened, unidimensional role (such as breadwinner or sex object or mother or father). So one's partner is experienced in a multidimensional way. One is comfortable with, even perhaps energized by, the fact that one's lover plays many roles and wears many proverbial hats. This encourages a wider repertoire of relatedness. One's partner is sometimes a quietly benign presence who allows others in the family to take center stage. At other times, one plays a more central role, lending a more directive hand. When one is vulnerable or down, one's spouse is nurturing and supportive. At other times when one is stuck, one's partner is challenging and even confrontational. At still other times, the couple are engaged in an active collaboration.

The capacity to see one's spouse as one's best friend does not preclude treating him or her as an accomplice engaged in illicit pleasure, as one's protector, or as nurturing. This fosters trust and aliveness, depth and excitement. Something in a relationship may be missing if one sees one's partner as only maternal or paternal or as simply a nurturer or protector.

Different types of love then flourish in the "same" relationship. At some moments there is a carnal fusion in which boundaries between the lovers are crossed and their identities feel merged. In other situations there is a loving connection between them, but there is also a great deal of psychological separateness. At still other moments, the love is concupiscent—desire rules and one takes rather than gives. At other times there is what Aristotle termed a *philia* sort of love: a deep, loving friendship in which one appreciates the other rather than desires to possess the other and the lovers are not fused or submerged in each other.[39]

The "psychopathology of potential space"[40] inhibits imaginative possibilities in a relationship because of the absence of a mutual interplay between reality and fantasy. This might occur when there is a dissociation of reality *or* fantasy, a foreclosure of imagination or a subsumption of reality to fantasy or fantasy to reality. In such an impoverished environment there is a shrinking of personal and interpersonal psychological space. Couples "think in either/or dichotomies . . . search for dominant/submissive relationships, and . . . perceive the world from uniquely subjective or objective perspectives."[41] There is a one-dimensional view of reality. Feelings, language, and interactions are treated as concrete, and one cannot hold a complex, ambiguous, or paradoxical idea without banishing one aspect or the other.[42]

A couple that "lives" in such an atmosphere relate in a closed, preordained, rigid, "perverse," and sterile way. Narrow ways of experiencing prevail and their relational repertoire is restricted. They do not accept differences—in fact they pathologize them, viewing them as irreconcilable. They polarize and split apparent oppositions such as intimacy and autonomy, security and risk, passion and reflectiveness, often defending one against the other. One quality is treated as the favored one, the superior way to be, and the second devalued and neglected. The couple may choose togetherness over time alone, or passion over reflectiveness. Risk seems the enemy of security; autonomy feels impossible in intimacy; and power seems inimical to trust. The couple then feels emotionally deprived, impoverished, and constrained.

Eros is depicted in literature and mythology as Janus-faced: as a provocateur and "mischief maker" as well as a source of universal cohesion.[43] It is at once chaotic and tantalizing, generative and healing. It fosters ecstacy and anguish. A loving relationship contains apparently contradictory qualities such as passion and reflectiveness, intimacy and autonomy, and security and risk. When integrated in a relationship, these ordinary polarities are mutually enriching. This creates an atmosphere conducive to openness, depth, and creativity.

Death exists amid life, yin is no less important than yang, and to know good one must have experienced evil. Integrating opposites has, I suspect, a ring of simplicity. It seems easy to do. But it is, I believe, *deceptively* complex—one of the hardest tasks in the world.

A central lesson of Stoic philosophers, Taoism, Jung, and Derrida is this mutual interconnection and integration of apparent polarities. Stoic philosophers of antiquity[44] asserted the interdependence or mutual entailment of the virtues (*antakolouthis*). Honesty without compassion breeds cruelty. Security without risk generates complacency and staleness. Courage needs moderation, prudence requires justice, the strengthening of will requires surrender as well as assertion.

Modell[45] has suggested that the acceptance of paradox is a higher developmental level of object relatedness. From the perspective that Modell is offering, the qualities that are seemingly opposed in love—intimacy and autonomy, passion and reflectiveness, loyalty and dissent—are actually mutually reinforcing and enriching.

There are many tones and colors in the symphony of love that need to be played in harmony. Most people would agree that connectedness to and engagement with one's partner constitute a central aspect of a loving relationship. Without relatedness, partners are detached, resembling two parallel but separated and segregated planets, each following their own orbit and never touching. But connectedness without autonomy and individuation impedes intimacy, for merger without independence can lead to engulfment that erodes individuality. One then drowns or is swallowed up in the other person and experiences a sense of self-dissolution. When each partner is not individuated, the relationship is then impoverished. Still, too much autonomy can foster impressive solos in which the other person is a mere accompanist not a participant in a beautiful duet. Crucial to intimacy is the recognition that one's partner is a separate and equivalent center of experience and initiative, who is to be experienced as a subject, in their own right. As Benjamin[46] notes, equally important is cultivating the capacity for self-assertion.

In a romantic space in a passionate relationship, such virtues can be integrated and serve one another because they are not seen as separate or opposed. One experiences this not by seeking a comfortable via media or middle way that rejects both extremes of apparent polarities, but rather by an active, vital, engagement in which both are encompassed and work together. A passage in E. M. Forster's *Howard's End* illustrates the point. It involves Margaret Schlegel's reflections after she has decided to marry Mr. Wilcox: "The businessman who assumes that this life is everything, and the mystic who asserts that it is nothing, fail, on this side and on that, to hit the truth. 'Yes, I see dear; it's about halfway between,' Aunt Juley had hazarded in earlier years. No; truth, being alive, was not halfway between anything. It was only to be found by continuous excursions into either realm, and though proportion is the final secret, to espouse it at the outset is to insure sterility."[47] Forster's misconstrual of the world-affirming (not renouncing) mystic notwithstanding, he illuminates this idea about integrating opposites. And "though proportion is the final secret," we cannot say beforehand what that would look like.

Let's briefly consider loyalty and 'disloyalty' in a loving relationship. Loyalty—that is, an unquestioned commitment to one's partner—is essential to a loving relationship. It is the glue that fosters safety and trust. But too much loyalty can be dangerous. It can breed blind obedience, myopia, and an evasion of ethical responsibility, for example when a parent doesn't protect a child against a sadistic spouse.

There are individuals in relationships—perhaps even loving ones—who are psychologically restricted and submerged because their devotion to their partner precludes any concern for their own feelings and needs. But there are moments when a relationship is best served by what Winnicott[48] termed "experimentation with disloyalty," by which he meant not sexual or emotional infidelity, but the capacity to question, challenge, and even dissent from one's partner so as to perceive and act in original and innovative ways. Experimenting with disloyalty may, at times, be affirming for both members of a couple and the relationship as a whole. Of course, the healthy proportions of loyalty and disloyalty need to be ascertained on an individual basis. This is true of all the interlacing qualities: passion and reflectiveness, security and risk, and intimacy and autonomy.

"But Love has pitched his mansion in/the place of excrement" the poet W. B. Yeats reminds us in "Crazy Jane Talks with the Bishop."[49] Love is never a "final presence," as Ulanov and Ulanov[50] aptly note. The final facet of creating a loving space in a relationship entails learning to work with difficulties, which sometimes includes what disgusts us.

There is a powerful tendency for many of us to conceive of such things as intimacy and love in an idealistic way, and our utopian picture hides the ubiquitous reality of imperfections and fallibility. We often assume that our or our partner's imperfections, not our ideals, are the culprit. Rather than question those ideals, we blame ourselves (or our spouse) for our failure to experience continuous love.

Creating a loving relationship entails living through and transforming what Thoreau would term the "quiet desperation" that accompanies the journey of most lovers—the struggles with dashed hopes and failures, unfulfilled ambitions, and sometimes even bitter resignation, amid blissful union and joyous discovery. Because reality rarely lives up to the promise of our fantasied hopes, coping with unloving feelings and fantasies is also crucial for sustaining a loving relationship. Patience, tolerance, and humor are, I believe, crucial to do this.

"To fall in love," suggests Jorges Luis Borges, "is to create a religion that has a fallible God."[51] Love is a religion in several senses. It is something awesome and majestic that has ultimate significance in one's life. It is something that one believes in deeply and passionately. One is devoted to it. It provides meaning and direction and orients one's life. *Religere* means to bind or connect. A loving relationship unites and binds one to another, thereby offering connectedness and solace as one is freed from the prison of isolated, encapsulated selfhood. Love is a religion with a *fallible* god, in that along with its immense power, it is all-too-humanly imperfect and flawed. It does not provide certain answers or unerring protection. It does not solve all one's dilemmas. It does not offer insurance against loneliness and suffering and loss. Lovers still are left with heart-wrenching choices and excruciating moral decisions and, in the case of the death of a spouse, cavernous voids.

Everything in nature, according to Santayana, is lyrical in its essence, comic in its existence, and tragic in its fate. Psychoanalysis has traditionally illuminated comic and tragic facets of love, the obstacles to it, and its wayward flights. By also elucidating what nourishes love—thereby fostering the emergence of its lyrical side—psychoanalysis might enlarge our capacity to imagine and experience love's range and possibilities.

Psychoanalysis has a twofold contribution to make to twenty-first century reflections on love: It can cultivate the qualities that nurture a loving environment in a relationship and illuminate and lessen the obstacles to experiencing it. Psychoanalysis teaches us that we need to think about love in a very different way from how we ordinarily do. Depictions of 'love' that pervade popular culture—movies, television, rap—are simplified and debased, conveying a distorted and dangerous view of what it is and how it is acquired and sustained. The search for love does not entail, as so-called reality television shows suggest, a battle between attractive and cunning people competing against one another as they struggle to 'win' the love of a wealthy, handsome man or a very beautiful woman. Love is not an instantaneous discovery of a person we have never met and have no history with who matches our idealized picture ("I looked across the room and knew s/he was the one"). Nor is it a permanently ecstatic feeling we have toward such a figure.

The implication of the psychoanalytic perspective that I have sketched in this chapter is that love is, as Fromm[52] recognized, an "art," a deeply meaningful experience available to those with emotional compatibility and physical chemistry, requiring commitment and self-awareness, discipline and practice, empathy and imagination. By illuminating the psychology of romantic space, the fact that love is an ambience or atmosphere that is cocreated by two people, who can either nurture and sustain it or neglect and deplete it, psychoanalysis increases our capacity to experience and nurture a loving relationship.

The couple—each loved and beloved—are unique and unclassifiable[53] as well as definable and predictable. Since love entails mystery as well as certainty, questions as well as answers, I hope my exploration of the psychological ingredients that nourish a loving relationship stirs the reader's passions about the subject and prompts his or her reflections and questions, critique and elaborations. Because as W. H. Auden said in the first edition of his poem "September 1st 1939": "We must love one another or perish."[54]

CHAPTER FOUR

There's More Than Meets the I

PSYCHOANALYTIC REFLECTIONS ON SPIRITUALITY

There is another world and it is in this one.
—Paul Eluard

To any vision must be brought an eye adapted to
what is to be seen.
—Plotinus

SEVERAL TIMES IN THE PAST YEAR prospective patients have indicated in their initial sessions with me that they seek a "spiritually oriented" therapist. During a recent consultation, a patient, whom I will call Joan, informed me that she was seeking therapy because she would like to encourage her "spiritual side" to emerge. She indicated that "spiritual" for her referred to an outlook on the universe that was not materialistic and valued the uniqueness of the individual and greater authenticity, personal centeredness, balance, and wisdom.

There has been a resurgence of interest in religion and spirituality in our world. Charismatic preachers assault the airwaves, fundamentalist ministers shape local and national politics, there are television programs on angels and the afterlife, *New York Times Magazine* cover stories on God, and *Newsweek* articles on the search for the sacred. The yearning for spirituality transcends organized

61

religion and spans all walks of life. The word "spirituality" appears with increasing frequency in books on the best-seller lists, in the media, and on television— and even in that bastion of Enlightenment science and rationalism, psychoanalysis. The word "spirituality" arises with greater frequency in the last few years in psychoanalytic articles, conferences, and books.[1] But these writings have not been integrated into psychoanalysis. They are more like stray notes than a central motif.

Even though I have practiced meditation and yoga for over twenty-six years and written a book on psychoanalysis and Buddhism (which Joan apparently did not know about), I was taken by surprise by the spirituality that she sought. The surprise was not because psychoanalytic treatment can't aid contemplative pursuits—I have personally and professionally witnessed the way that it can—but because her quest to experience spiritual facets of herself was so incongruent with the pervasive pathologizing of religion and the shunning of spirituality in the first one hundred years of psychoanalysis.

Ever since Freud, drawing on a secular Enlightenment agenda underwritten by the privileging of reason and science, critiqued religion as an illusion designed to allay one's vulnerability and helplessness in the face of the terrors of the universe,[2] psychoanalysts have either neglected or pathologized religion and spiritual experience. We psychoanalysts are usually anti (or un) spiritual, unreflectively approaching spiritual matters with antipathy, naiveté, or skepticism.[3] We assume that spirituality is delusive or misguided; a regressive urge for unity with the preoedipal mother, a wooly search for false and illusory salvations, a self-centered withdrawal from the world, or voluntary self-hypnosis.[4]

Helene Deutsch considered her treatment of a nun less than a complete cure because she couldn't convert her. Otto Fenichel maintained that every successful psychoanalysis results in the termination of religious belief. While not all psychoanalysts have pathologized spiritual experiences—witness the work of Jung, Fromm, Horney, Kelman, Milner, Ulanov, Bion, Kovel, Ghent, Symington, Roland, Grotstein, Eigen, Jones, Sorenson, Corbett, Cooper, Finn, Marcus, Magid, and so forth—many have. Jung[5] even went so far as to claim that the absence of a "religious outlook"—which included spiritual experiences—leads to neurosis, which flies in the face of the positivistic epistemology and the Enlightenment distrust of religion that has deeply shaped psychoanalysis. Spirituality, not sexuality, aggression, gender, or even race, may thus be the unconscious of psychoanalysis.

An experience I had playing basketball thirty-three years ago, along with subsequent personal and clinical experiences, suggest the essential inadequacy of the taken-for-granted psychoanalytic neglect or pathologization of the spiritual. There is, as I hope to imply in this chapter, *more than meets the I.*

The memory almost three decades later remains vivid: It was February 1971, Riverdale, New York. I was a senior point guard on my high school's basketball team. We were playing an away league game against a team whom we were favored to beat and to remain in contention for the league title we had to win this game. When we scored a basket with about ten seconds remaining, our victory appeared, like our adolescence, invincible. Our one-point lead seemed to be sealed. But when someone on the opposing team hit a shot with six seconds to go we suddenly felt buried alive.

Five seconds remained after we called time-out. Our huddle was like a UN meeting without an interpreter. I remember circumventing the chaos and moving next to my coach. I stood quite close to him and asked him to tell my teammates not to panic and to get me the ball. He did. The other team lined up about ninety feet down the court near our basket. One of my teammates took the ball out of bounds and rolled it to me near mid court, approximately forty-five feet away. The clock didn't start until I touched the ball. As I scooped the ball up, turned, and began dribbling up the left side of the court with my left hand I seemed to enter a realm where the game and I were not-two. Time appeared to slow down and elongate. The gym seemed silent. I didn't hear the roar of the crowd or feel the cold of the gym. I felt no pressure. I also felt no fear. Hope and dread, victory and defeat did not exist. As I approached the top of the key I sensed it was time to shoot. I wrapped my left hand around the middle of the ball, my fingertips touching its seams, my right hand cradling the top right corner. I squared my shoulders to the basket, bent my knees, and jumped in the air. I scanned the basket with a dispassionate gaze, like an archer studying the target before releasing the arrow. My left hand was extended, right through the fingertips. Just as my left hand released the ball and my left wrist waved to the rim, the arms of my 6' 2" defender enveloped me. I could no longer see the rim. As my feet touched the wooden gymnasium floor there was a cavernous silence. A deafening roar broke my spell and spectators from our side of the gym mobbed the court. It was only then that I glanced at the scoreboard and realized that my shot had gone in and that we had won the game by one point.

The locker room was noisy but I was strangely quiet, unmoved by the dramatic win and my personal heroics. I wasn't numb. Nor was I indifferent to winning; as a highly competitive teenage athlete, winning was very important to me. The victory did not lose its luster because I was upset by the transience of the sweetness of victory. No. I was unemotional about our comeback because victory paled compared to what I had internally experienced. I remember standing alone in the dim, smelly high school locker room after my teammates had showered and changed, replaying what I had experienced the last five seconds of the game: the heightened attentiveness, focus, and clarity. The way time seemed to expand. The absence of thought, pressure, and fear. The serenity.

Before those last five seconds of the game I would have called my childhood irreligious. While my teammates were celebrating our narrow victory at the end of the game, I was preoccupied with the tantalizing glimpse I had of another domain of being, what I would later term spirituality or the sacred, in which I was open to the moment without a sense of time, unself-conscious but acutely aware, highly focused and engaged, yet relaxed and without fear.

What I experienced at the end of that game had a deep and lasting impression on me and became a defining moment in my life. I don't know if astrophysicists feel a radical transformation and expansion of their own world when they discover alternative universes. After the conclusion of that basketball game, I knew directly and viscerally that there was a radically different way of experiencing oneself and relating to the world than I had ever been taught or exposed to. The vice grip of ambition, victory, competitiveness, and succeeding at all costs—the divinities I worshiped until the last five seconds of that game—was loosened. I now saw them as false idols. While winning still felt better than losing, the joy of just playing the game became as important as winning. Zero-sum games in which to have a winner you must have a loser were less interesting to me. I was endlessly taught as a male in the United States that willful effort was one of the highest virtues. I still valued and recognized the importance of trying to make things happen. But I experienced at the end of that basketball game the way unself-consciousness and self-forgetfulness, as well as self-assertion, are crucial to a human life. It was now clear to me that surrendering to and flowing with life is no less important than planning and goal-directed behavior.

Various psychological and spiritual explanations have been offered for changes in the self's boundaries and contours ranging from Freud's[6] pathologizing of "oceanic" experiences to Eastern contemplative claims that the spiritual quest is an expansion of the self so that it opens to and even merges with the world it is embedded in. Ordinarily these different perspectives are treated as *oppositional* rather than potentially *cross-pollinating*. Spiritual experiences and psychological ones, from my perspective, *are* different *and* potentially enriching rather than irreconcilable facets of being.

In this chapter I reflect upon how spiritual experiences might enrich psychoanalysis and how psychoanalysis might enlighten spiritual seekers. My thesis is twofold: (1) both psychoanalysis and the spiritual quest have been impoverished by the lack of contact between them and (2) both could be enriched by a dialogue of reciprocity in which there is mutual respect, a recognition of differences, and a willingness to learn from each other. Insights from spiritual experiences could expand psychoanalytic conceptions of the nature of self-experience, empathy, and compassion. Experiencing spirituality can lead to an enlargement of consciousness and an enrichment of one's world.[7] A secular psychoanalytic perspective that resists spiritual experiences is impoverished, disenchanting the world and robbing it of its wonder, mystery, and splendor. But there is a tendency outside psychoanalysis to idealize spiritual experiences as blissful and inherently positive. Psychoanalysis reveals the fallacy of romanticizing these experiences and can elucidate pathologies of spirit.

My strategy will be to first contextualize the burgeoning interest in spirituality in contemporary culture. Then I will discuss spiritual dimensions of psychoanalysis. In the third section I explore psychoanalysis's neglect of the spiritual and the cost to psychoanalysis. Then I examine pathologies of spirit. Next I consider some clinical implications of valuing spiritual experiences. In the concluding section I point toward some of the ingredients of a contemplative psychoanalysis, a psychoanalysis that would at once be receptive to, yet properly critical of, spirituality.

There may be at least three reasons for the heightened interest in spirituality in our age: modernization, secularization, and postmodernism. The word modernity refers to a period since the Renaissance that is separated from the preceding historical epoch by the "Copernican revolution, Newtonian physics, Cartesian epistemology and metaphysics, humanism and its political revolutions, and the beginning of the technological, industrial and commercial transformations of society."[8] The modern world became, in part, secularized and despiritualized, by which I mean that, external reality and subjective reality have been increasingly experienced psychologically and nonspiritually.[9] There has been a desecularization of the world in recent years. The contemporary world is furiously religious except for Swedes and "elective Swedes"—namely, intellectuals, professionals, therapists, lawyers, doctors, scientists, and engineers. There hasn't, however, always been a corresponding reenchantment of the universe.[10]

What we have lost to secularization may outweigh the potential gain in self-awareness and personal responsibility. Religious worldviews or frameworks of understanding the universe are no longer compelling for the vast majority of people the way they used to be prior to the modern age. Secularization repudiated core values of religion.[11] Explicitly abjuring religion, psychoanalysis has forsaken questions of ultimate concern that are central to human well-being such as: "What is the purpose and meaning of human life?" A self-alienating worldview is unwittingly ushered in. Individuals feel cast adrift, disconnected from larger frameworks that explain conclusively the universe and our place within it. This breeds a pervasive sense of meaninglessness and alienation. Spirituality may fill a void generated by the failure of secular movements and theories and associated ways of living (such as positivism, rationalism, consumerism, hedonism, technological utopianism, Freudianism, and Marxism) to give meaningful answers to questions of ultimate concern, including the nature of evil, goodness, suffering, love, death, and the meaning of life.

Many people in the West in the twenty-first century experience a rupture and critical distance from the culturally shared consciousness and sensibility that shaped the modern world. There is a growing recognition that we now live in a very different world from our modernist predecessors, which is usually termed "postmodern." Postmodernism is heterogeneous and protean rather than a singular essence. But there is a general consensus that it challenges certain common foundations and beliefs about knowledge, truth, reality, authority, and selves of the modernist world.

In deabsolutizing many of the givens and foundations of our modernist universe from objective knowledge and unimpeachable authority, to linguistic reference and absolute political sovereignty, postmodernism has undermined the assumptive framework that structured our world and shed new light on oppression and the hidden exercise of power. Postmodernistic writings, at their best, remind us of the neglected voices and oppressed/suppressed stories and voices within a narrative or theory. The voices of the disenfranchised are more readily heard.

But postmodern thought has also left wreckage in its wake. Deconstructing the foundations of our customs and traditions and the binding cultural and symbolic meanings and understandings that undergird our social and personal worlds—without replacing them with something substantial and viable—leaves us deeply unsettled, even psychologically "homeless."

The postmodern relativization of values makes it more difficult to consider questions of morality. When there are no foundations for concepts and values; when all values are underwritten by desire and the will to power, then there is an ethical void. A burgeoning concern with spirituality may also fill a moral vacuum ushered in by the pervasive evasion of values and ethics within postmodern thought (Claude Barbre, personal communication, 1998).

The rising interest in spirituality may be an antidote to the estrangement of humans from self and nature caused by Western culture in general as well as postmodernism in particular. The belief that humans and nature are different, discontinuous, and separate is a central facet of Western culture. Humans are trained to believe that they are superior to nature. They treat it as territory that they can colonize. Western culture also overvalues reason and logic and examines phenomena by dismantling and dissecting it into it parts, rather than studying it whole or in context. These facets of Western culture foster an alienating mode of being; separating humans from each other, themselves, their bodies, their feelings, and nature.

"Thought is born of failure," suggests the British physicist and philosopher L. L. Whyte. "When our actions are fulfilling, there is nothing extraneous to bother with."[12] The contemporary resurgence of interest in spirituality can be seen as a reminder of neglected facets of our Western heritage and our being. Spirituality, according to the empirical research of Batson and Ventis, "has positive correlations with mental health defined as freedom from guilt and worry, presence of well-being and social links, creative productivity, subjective unification and organization, self-control, flexibility, and open-mindedness."[13] Spirituality may be an antidote to the alienation of Western civilization. We might not be so interested in spirituality at this historical juncture if our lives felt more connected and meaningful.

Defining and explaining what we mean by the words "spirituality" and "sacred" is a difficult task. The dictionary defines "spiritual" as "not tangible or material"—that is, beyond sense impressions and perhaps ineffable. The "spiritual" is often contrasted with the psychological as well as the material, the mundane, and the flesh.

Spiritual writing has taken numerous forms including Attic Greek dialogues, works of biblical scholarship, poetry, metaphysical tracts, Zen cookbooks, Kabbalistic texts, and psychospiritual self-help manuals. Whether these writings are confessional, prescriptive, satirical, or polemical, they often share at least some interest in questions of ultimate meaning and concern—who we are, why we are here, what is the meaning and purpose of our existence, and how we should live—that are often not addressed in the research lab, the opinion poll, and sometimes even on the analytic couch.

The meaning of a word, Wittgenstein[14] reminds us, is its "use in the language." Several years ago, curious about the meaning of spirituality, I began jotting down the variety of ways patients in treatment used the word "spirituality." There were a cluster of overlapping meanings and uses. It always referred to something positive: for example, Martin Luther King Jr. or Mother Theresa or the Dalai Lama, who were presumed to exhibit unusual compassion or wisdom. It never connoted anything negative. When Freud stated in the opening paragraph of *Civilization and Its Discontent* that "people commonly use false standards of measurement—that they seek power, success, and wealth for themselves and admire them in others, and that they underestimate what is of true value in life"[15]—he was pointing toward what we might term a spiritual vision of the universe, even if he did not use that language or consciously believe in that category.[16] The word "spirituality" was used by patients in five different ways. It expressed a deeply felt sense of unity and connection with the universe. One surrenders control and self-interest and opens to the world; the gap between self and universe lessens and one experiences the divineness of life and a serenity of being. The second use of the word spirituality depicted deeper, more sustaining values guiding one's life—higher meaning and purpose than self-aggrandizement—and a more balanced, flexible, and tolerant attitude toward life. The cultivation of particular qualities and virtues that are ordinarily neglected in daily life in Western secular culture such as awe, wonder, humility, forgiveness, joyousness, love, wisdom, and compassion were closely linked to the third use of the word spirituality. The word was also used by patients to refer to a better, more humble, alive, contented, and loving self; or an unconditioned and uncorrupted, pure, and authentic core of one's being and a natural and organic way of living, devoid of artifice and dissembling. And finally: Spiritual paths referred to the practices designed to foster any of the first four experiences.

And yet, despite the salutary facets of spirituality, it has been pathologized or neglected in much of psychoanalysis. A variety of reasons explain this.

Spirituality is most frequently spoken about in religious circles and contexts. Religion, according to Freud, offers illusory consolations in the face of the vicissitudes of life. It has also been guilty of numerous "crimes" and "misdemeanors,"[17] including acts of intolerance, violence, and oppression toward dissenting viewpoints and alternative religions.

There are more personal reasons why Freud dismissed religion. Freud had a deeply problematic relationship with his mother that he completely denied and disavowed.[18] In fact, he consciously idealized her. He described the mother–son relationship (in a strikingly un/pre-Freudian formulation) as completely free of conflict and ambivalence. The disavowed dimensions of his struggles with his mother shaped and skewed his views on women. There is evidence that Freud unconsciously connected and conflated religion and the feminine.[19] His dismissal of religion was, I believe, deeply influenced by his negative and mystifying experiences with the latter.

The third reason for spirituality's dismissal in psychoanalysis was that James Strachey's English translation of Freud's German was shaped and confined by positivistic assumptions, which gave a scientized sense to Freud's humanistic insights and made the spirit seem even less germane to psychoanalysis.[20] A soulless version of Freud's work could not address or illuminate the spiritual. And finally, exploring the domain of spirituality foregrounds the question Winnicott recognized that psychoanalysis—with its essentially "tragic" worldview,[21] its acknowledgment of the inescapable mysteries, afflictions, and losses permeating human existence—has rarely addressed: "What is life about, apart from illness?"

Psychoanalysis has suffered because of its neglect of spirituality. The cost of a psychoanalysis that neglects or eclipses the sacred is that it embraces a secular modernist/postmodernist worldview in which the individual is disconnected from larger sources of meaning and solace. Individuals are left unmoored and disconnected when they are not embedded in something beyond the isolated, unencumbered self. The individual, in a secular world, is a god-term—the ultimate ground of being and source of meaning. Freud[22] claimed that to question the meaning of life is a sign of emotional illness. But the search for meaning—which is a central (although not exclusive) property of the spiritual life—may enrich one's life and be life-affirming rather than defensive.[23]

To not question the meaning of life can inadvertently lead to being attached to meaninglessness, thereby fostering alienation and anomie and compromising one's emotional health. From such a secular perspective, life is disenchanted, emptied of wonder, awe, sublimity, and sacredness. The alienation of many patients (and therapists) may not be unrelated to such a disconnection from the world in which psychoanalysis is embedded. Various substitutes are then consciously or unconsciously recruited to ground the disconnected individual. The self and the theories and organizations we are affiliated with, for example, may be treated as idols, which theologian Reinhold Niebuhr defines as "absolutizing the relative," by which he means making a particular, local, partial truth into a universally valid one. Making the individual the ground of being leads to an excessively egocentric conception of self-experience. When the isolated individual is the ultimate source of meaning, then altruism and self-centeredness are seen as dichotomized rather than intimately interpenetrating. There is a greater attachment to our theories and a lack of tolerance and civility in psychoanalytic institutions, especially toward those with differing points of view.

To see the self-centered psychoanalytic view of self, reflect for a moment on the differences between Martin Buber's view of relationships and those of many relational thinkers (Benjamin is a notable exception). The latter view the other in terms of what it did or did not provide the self. The other is then seen not as a subject with its own unique needs but, to use the language of Klein, as a need-gratifying object. The relationship between self and other, as I suggested previously, is reduced to an instrumental one with the crucial question being: "What did I get (or not get) from the other?" Buber, on the other hand, stresses a *moral* relation with the other, asking what can I give to the other, not simply what the other can do for me. The other is seen in Buber as a subject or a thou with his or her own needs and ideals.

With the notion of the depressive position, Kleinian thought offers a vision of self-experience that goes beyond the egocentric version that permeates many psychoanalytic conceptualizations of self. In the depressive position the other is experienced as a whole and separate person. One feels guilt and the urge for reparation toward other people because of the damage or hurt one has inflicted.

Let us return for a moment to my epiphany playing basketball. Or you could reflect on mundane or extraordinary experiences that you may have had playing a musical instrument, painting, solving a scientific conundrum, communing with nature, whitewater rafting, or making love. As barriers between self and not-self erode in the "nonself-centered subjectivity"[24] one embodies in moments of spirituality, one feels aligned with the universe—a self-expansive and self-enriching connectedness with the world characterized by a sense of engagement, not escape or detachment. In this being-at-oneness, one views the world from a more inclusive perspective in which self and other are seen as mutually interpenetrating facets of the universe rather than as polar oppositions. Seeing the world and one's self from this perspective casts a different, more benign light on such perennial human struggles as anxiety, guilt, fear, and the possibility for happiness and inner peace. Spiritual experiences suggest that there is more to life than the depressive position. I'd like to suggest that nonself-centered subjectivity, experiences of spirituality, are a fourth state of being that is different from and transcends the autistic/contiguous, paranoid/schizoid, and depressive positions that Klein and Ogden elucidate.[25] One is not at war with oneself or the other. Self and other exist in a nondualistic relationship that may be devoid of conflict, guilt, and fear. One is in a philia or friendship rather than adversarial relationship with oneself in most spiritual experiences. While afflictive states of mind such as strife and trepidation are often absent in moments of spiritual experience, negative experiences such as self-nullifying fusion with and compliance to another may be present. More on this later.

Psychoanalysis neglects the sacred, as well as spirituality and nonself-centered subjectivity. A world without spirit is secularized, emptied of wonder and awe, bleached of mystery and radiance, sublimity and splendor. Psycho-analysis needs to be receptive to the sacred.

The profusion of analysands and analysts who are exploring spiritual prac-tice and the increasing number of analytic conferences and articles on psycho-analysis and spirituality suggest that we may be witnessing a hunger for and a return of the spiritually repressed in contemporary psychoanalysis.[26] More than five hundred therapists and spiritual seekers, for example, attended a conference in 1994 in New York City on "Healing the Suffering Self: A Dialogue among Psychoanalysts and Buddhists" sponsored by two psychoanalytic institutes. One of the reasons that increasing numbers of people are turning away from psy-choanalysis may be its secular psychology, not simply managed care or the anti-analytic contemporary cultural climate. Might many analysands and analysts turn to the meditative cushion or the yoga ashram because psychoanalysis does not fully nurture their spiritual needs or hunger?

THE SPIRIT(UALITY) OF PSYCHOANALYSIS

While psychoanalysis has certainly been tardy in appreciating spirituality—often either pathologizing or disavowing it—spiritual experiences have been present in psychoanalysis since its inception. We do not need to "bring spiritu-ality into psychoanalysis" because it has always been there.[27] Let me briefly mention several examples. Horney, Kelman, Bion, and myself have noted the resonances between meditation and psychoanalytic listening.[28] Freud's[29] delin-eation of the optimal state of mind to listen—evenly hovering attention, care-ful, moment-to-moment awareness of whatever we are experiencing—shares two important features with Eastern meditative practices.[30] In Freud's method, one gives oneself over to and surrenders to experience that one attends to with all one's being. In her posthumously published *Final Lectures,* Horney[31] discusses how Buddhism can train "wholehearted attentiveness" or absorption in what one is doing such as analytic listening. "Wholehearted attentiveness" is a pre-requisite for doing sound analytic work and is, according to Horney, a "rare attainment,"[32] a faculty for which Orientals have a much deeper feeling than we do . . . [and] a much better training."[33] Harold Kelman,[34] a close associate of Horney and a past president of the American Academy of Psychoanalysis, rec-ognized this feature of psychoanalytic method when he asserted that, carried to its logical conclusion, it is Eastern in technique but not in theory. According to Kelman, the theories underlying psychoanalysis and Eastern thought are different, but Eastern meditative techniques can enrich psychoanalytic practice.

Bion[35] attempted to elaborate on Freud's perspectives on listening in his recommendation that analysts listen without "memory," "desire," or "understanding."[36] He believed that this kind of listening promotes being a *real* self. It also resonates with Buddhist meditative practices, embodying what contemporary Buddhists term "beginner's mind." In the mind of the beginner "there are many possibilities," notes Zen teacher Shunryu Suzuki, "but in the expert's there are few."[37]

Lacan's obscure and elusive style of writing may function, as Mitchell and Black aptly note, like a Zen koan,[38] those enigmatic and rationally unsolvable conundrums that teachers of Zen give to their students in an attempt to foster the open presence and receptivity of "beginner's mind." Challenging ordinary, habitual preconceptions and ways of perceiving and thinking, as Lacan's writing does, can sometimes generate a transformed perspective and new emotional insights and understandings.

In my own clinical and personal experience, an ongoing practice of meditation fosters an uncongealed mind that cultivates a greater capacity to free-associate and be attuned to the nuances of one's inner experience including countertransference. Greater personal freedom, playfulness, and creativity are by-products. Ferenczi intimates the salutary facets of these subtle and not always tangible free-associational experiences when he suggestively remarks that you don't free-associate in order to be cured, you are cured when you can free-associate,[39] which I believe points toward an unfettered, Taoist way of being, in which one flows with, rather than fights against, the currents of life.

Emmanuel Ghent usefully distinguished between "submission" and "surrender." Submission is a self-negating "submergence of self" in, and bondage to, the other.[40] It is a masochistic corruption and distortion or "perversion" and "defensive mutant" of surrender.[41] Surrender is not resignation or "defeat," but a self-enriching, yielding liberation and expansion of self as one opens to the larger world one is embedded in. Surrender fosters a greater harmony and flowing with life.

The "religious" attitude, according to Jung, involved not belief in a "creed," but "careful and scrupulous observation" of the "'numinosum,'"[42] an awe-inspiring experience that fills one with blissful exaltation. It is an encounter with an unsurpassable value to which absolute respect is due. Religion designates, for Jung, "the attitude peculiar to a consciousness which has been altered by the experience of the numinosum."[43] And spirituality is the search for meaning in one's life. With its careful examination of an analysand's life in the service of generating meaning and facilitating his or her uniqueness, psychoanalysis embodies this quest.

Winnicott's[44] "transitional phenomena" and "transitional space," a fertile, creative state of being and an environment that is neither self nor nonself but both, depicts (without exhausting) the psychic space in which spiritual experiences (and creative ones) occur, as I suggested in chapter one. A transitional phenomena is not an internal or external object or possession. It is a third part of a human being, an "intermediate area of *experiencing*,"[45] between the "subjective and the objectively perceived,"[46] that is neither inner psychic reality nor external reality but to which each contributes. Winnicott notes that it's "inherent in art and religion."[47] From Winnicott we might learn that moments of what we term spiritual experience are not possessions or commodities or achievements of the self, but experiences that arise in the intersection and interaction of self and world. Such experiences partake of both but belong to neither.

And finally, psychoanalysis can be a sacred space, a sanctuary for raising the deepest sorts of questions about how we might live.[48] Having the opportunity of hearing another person's deepest sufferings and yearnings is sacred. There are certain moments in treatment—perhaps when the analytic dyad is highly attuned and synergistic, playing emotional or mental jazz—when it feels as if something sacred is happening in the consulting room.[49]

THE PSYCHOANALYSIS OF SPIRIT: PSYCHOPATHOLOGY OF SPIRITUALITY IN EVERYDAY LIFE

> Even of Holiness
> there is offal:
> Just as there is sweat
> and hair and excrement,
> So Holiness too
> has its offal.
> —Nachman of Bratzlav

Spirituality is usually presented as an antidote to the rampant narcissism in personal, corporate, and political relations that permeates and plagues our world. Going "beyond narcissism" is unreflectively accepted by many people as a viable solution to the egocentricity that afflicts us individually and as a culture.[50]

The plethora of scandals in spiritual communities in recent years involving esteemed "masters" illegally expropriating funds from the communities and sexually exploiting students[51] suggests that the idealization of spiritual experiences can be harmful because there are sometimes hidden dangers.[52] Illusions and pitfalls abound on the spiritual path. The pursuit of spirituality rarely stands up to the pure image we have of an individual attempting to reach a higher plane of awareness and understanding. Instead, it may be used to bypass, circumvent, or attempt to heal emotional trauma. It can allow us to avoid conflict that we would be better off dealing directly with, or forestall growth by masking developmental arrests or lacunae.

Spiritual literature acknowledges hazards on the spiritual path ranging from sloth and torpor to pride and anger. For example, Buddhism terms these and other afflictive energies the ten "impediments,"[53] the ten "fetters,"[54] and the six "hindrances."[55] Learning to skillfully manage these obstacles is a crucial facet of Buddhist practice.[56] And yet, despite the fact that interferences play an indispensable role in the meditative process, they have been neglected and incompletely understood in the meditative literature. The classical[57] and contemporary Buddhist literature[58] has delineated many of the conscious personal and environmental interferences to meditation: "hindrances" (such as sense desire, anger, restlessness, sloth, and doubt); "impediments" (e.g., excessive involvement with projects and theoretical studies divorced from practice); and "fetters" (including attachment to blissful nonordinary states of consciousness, adherence to [wrongful] rites and ceremonies, ignorance, and self-centered thinking). The unconscious psychological and interpersonal obstacles to meditative practice, however, have not been systematically elaborated.[59]

There is a complex relationship between spirituality and psychopathology. Psychoanalysts have tended to reduce and flatten the complexity of the relation between them, conceiving of the two in singular and narrow ways. Within psychological circles, the psychological is traditionally treated as superior to the spiritual and the latter is then viewed as pathological. In religious literature and communities, spiritual experiences are presumed to be superior to psychological ones.

Roland usefully challenges and expands traditional psychoanalytic conceptions when he suggests that the "spiritual and normality/psychopathology" are "on two separate continua, intersecting and interacting in various ways."[60] The relationship between spirituality and psychology and psychopathology, from my perspective, is complex and multidimensional, differing depending on the changing contexts that characterize their relationship. It is best thought of as a fertile mosaic composed of diverse elements that are, at different moments, separate and distinct or overlapping and sometimes complementary or even synergistic. A double or triple helix might give a sense of what I am pointing toward. More specifically: There are times when spirituality and psychology are separate. There are therapists and patients, for example, who are self-aware and psychologically healthy and are not oriented toward the spiritual. And there are genuine spiritual seekers who are not interested in psychological matters.[61]

There are situations when the psychological and the spiritual dovetail and cross-pollinate. There are analysands who suffer, for example, from neglecting the realm of the spiritual. Spiritual practice could aid their own psychological development and health. Meditation can help patients and therapists attend with greater clarity and depth to their inner experience. It can also cultivate greater tolerance of affect and a more fluid and multidimensional and less narcissistic experience of self.[62] But there are psychological conflicts that sometimes impede one's spiritual quest. Psychoanalysis could aid spiritual seekers in resolving inner psychological issues and developmental arrests and gain insight into troubling transferences with their spiritual teachers. Resolving these emotional struggles could deepen their spiritual practice. Psychoanalytic understandings of the dynamics of interpersonal relationships could elucidate psychopathology in spiritual communities. From my perspective, psychoanalysis and spiritual traditions are both necessary for the art of living.

A great many people in Western civilization excessively worry about the future or torture themselves about the past and feel disconnected from the actual texture of their lives in the present. A heightened capacity to reside in the moment can lessen these destructive tendencies. But glorifying the wisdom of the moment can become a way of avoiding earlier trauma or conflictual or terrifying developmental crossroads. Even blissful oceanic experiences do not solve ethical dilemmas or the challenges of growing up and becoming a unique individual. The spiritual quest can be a defense against embodied living, against tackling life's basic issues and everyday problems, including loss, intimacy, alienation, getting out of a bad relationship, confronting a stagnating career, or coping with one's mortality.

In spiritual matters, as in real estate, practically no one voluntary trades down. If spiritual seekers believed that they would end up worse off because of their spiritual practices, they wouldn't pursue them. Zen teacher Shunryu Suzuki[63] speaks of "that gaining idea."

A psychoanalysis of spirit would attend to the hidden motivations and secondary gains of the spiritual quest as well as its exalted dimensions. Psychoanalysis could show that spirituality, like all human experience, has multiple meanings and serves multiple functions ranging from the adaptive and transformative to the defensive and psychopathological. Psychoanalytically informed reflections on spirituality could offer tools to deidealize spiritual experiences and elucidate pathologies and illusions of spirit. In working psychoanalytically with several Buddhists and students of yoga, a rabbi, numerous nondenominational spiritual seekers, and several spiritually inclined artists, I have observed a variety of pathologies of spirit including using the spiritual quest or spiritual experiences to narcissistically inflate oneself, evade subjectivity, deny emotional losses, shield one from the painful vicissitudes of everyday experience, and neglect ethical responsibility. The spiritual path has allowed its devotees to engage in masochistic surrender, schizoid detachment, and obsessional self-anesthetization, and to pathologically mourn traumatic experiences. I will briefly discuss several of these. Since my focus is highly selective, I provide illustrative examples rather than more fully fleshed out clinical interactions or vignettes.

As a jumping-off point for a consideration of the pathologies of spirit, consider a poem by Jane Kenyon: "Once, in my early thirties, I saw / that I was a speck of light in the great / river of light that undulates through time. / I was floating with the whole / human family. We were all colors—those / who are living now, those who have died, / those who are not yet born." The last six words of the concluding line of this poem awakened me out of the blessed, unitive tranquility the poem induced in me: "For a few / moments I floated, completely calm, / and I no longer hated having to exist."[64] Spiritual experiences for Jane Kenyon, as for most of us, can be used in the service of a variety of ends, ranging from the constructive to the defensive. Many spiritual seekers bypass or keep emotional conflict or turmoil at bay by immersion in oneness experiences.

Narcissism haunts our culture, generating self-inflation, ruthless self-centeredness, and intolerance and hard-heartedness toward those who suffer or are less fortunate. I have repeatedly observed a great deal of narcissism in people on the spiritual quest. While Buddhism offers a powerful critique of narcissism as well as strategies for addressing it, it may sometimes inadvertently foster rather than resolve self-disorders and egocentricity.

In *Psychotherapy and Buddhism* I discussed the attraction for one Buddhist, whom I called Albert, of the no-self doctrine of Buddhism. Albert was an affable humanities professor in his late twenties who suffered from conflicts over individuation and success, excessive self-judgment, diminished self-esteem, inauthenticity, compliance, and a pervasive sense of directionlessness and meaninglessness.

He was an only child who was raised as an agnostic. In the beginning of treatment Albert described his mother as caring and devoted. As treatment proceeded, other images of her emerged. He later saw her as a rigid person who was more concerned with everyone conforming to her view of reality, which included how her son should act and be. She was scared of feelings and was deeply committed to banishing all aspects of internal, subjective life. She demanded that everyone around her live in accordance with her narrow view of reality. Albert felt that she lived in a "fortune cookie" universe in which her "shoulds" were idealized. Clichéd responses ("You must have felt badly when you got that rejection") replaced genuine emotional engagement. Albert felt impactless and nonexistent in her presence. His mother was like a "fencer who parries everything I say." Instead of being affirmed and validated by her, he felt nonengaged and invisible.

Albert had a distant relationship with his father, whom he experienced as intelligent, detached, critical, and passive. His father submitted to his wife's way of living and relating and never sustained an interest in his son. Albert never felt understood or supported by him. Albert described a pervasive pattern with his parents of their laundering communication of all subjective meaning, trivializing his feelings, and nullifying his authentic subjectivity, while appearing to exude empathy and concern.

In Albert's view, his parents did not see him or themselves as subjects capable of introspecting, feeling, desiring, or playing. Rather, he was coerced into accommodating to their preexisting viewpoint on reality. To stay connected to his parents he had to hide his subjective life. He "harmonized" with their view of reality, so as to not feel "like an astronaut cut off from home base in outer space" because that was the only hope of being emotionally related to them.

His parents were sorely unresponsive to his inner reality and failed to encourage his uniqueness from emerging or flourishing. In fact, they supported compliance with their narrow mode of being by rewarding submissiveness and conventionality and discouraging authenticity and individuation. Albert developed a private subjective world of depth and richness, but he had great difficulty believing in its validity and sustaining his commitment to it. The price of conforming to his parents' wishes was to bury his own sense of how he should live. He kept alive the tenuous hope of being accepted by them by banishing huge parts of his self through subverting and obscuring his "voice." This led to an excessively limited view of himself and his capabilities. What *he* wanted lacked significance to him and he felt that his life was not his own. This left him directionless.

Because his subjectivity had been so profoundly erased by his parents he felt as if he had no subjective existence. He felt invisible in his family, with no voice and no impact. Albert was attracted to the no-self doctrine because it resonated with his experience of self-nullification. The self-evasion that Buddhism fostered for Albert was a defense against his own sense of nonbeing. Believing in the doctrine of no-self also rationalized away and artificially disavowed his sadness and grief about an unlived life. It is not that he didn't live or missed out on life; there is no subject to experience subjective existence. Several years ago a patient of mine who was a student of Zen said to me: "Psychoanalytic treatment helped me with *self*-realization, not *nonself* derealization."

Self-emptiness is often masked by the idealization of spiritual teachers or the divine as well as spiritual ideals of the voidness of reality. From self psychology we can learn that one momentarily derives strength from an identification with and a submission to an idealized spiritual teacher who is presumed to be unconditionally accepting and loving, never harsh, judgmental, or abandoning. Here a spiritual teacher, cause, ideology, or experience provides vital and missing functions to the self such as the guidance or direction or identification with idealized strength, calmness, or wisdom that one lacked from parents or surrogate caregivers. One's own personal deprivation and bereftness are thus denied and avoided.

In its most extreme versions, such surrender can unfortunately take the form of masochistic submission in which one may become pathologically deferential toward a spiritual teacher or in a spiritual community. Initially the uncritical devotion may feel relieving as it seems to offer connectedness and even direction about how to live. But one can observe over a longer period of time that the person does not think for him/herself, denies signs of groupthink, and rationalizes disturbing behavior on the part of either the teacher or members of the community. One's individuality is obliterated, not enriched. When the spiritual teacher is immune to feedback and the student has no impact, then authoritarianism is operative.[65] Questions that cannot be asked about the teacher or spiritual experiences or doctrines that are supposed to be completely taken on faith may signal the presence of a teacher or a spiritual community that is autocratic rather than liberatory.

Sometimes spiritual *experiences* rather than teachers are idealized. Experiences of oneness and bliss offered one meditator, a highly competent and successful middle-aged professional man, a way of avoiding, rather than confronting and coping with, the excruciating pain and sadness of his divorce.

Ron initiated therapy after his wife of twenty years announced that she wanted a divorce. He was stunned and felt that he was falling apart. Intelligent and articulate, Ron was a successful lawyer highly regarded in his field. He was an intense man, with a commanding presence and an incisive intellect. I felt as if there was little margin for error in our interactions. He instantaneously got on the offensive and treated me as if I was a hostile witness in a courtroom whenever I attempted to explore the realm of his feelings. Ron had been experiencing severe stress and the feeling he was "out of control" since his wife's sudden announcement, which he had been trying to handle by meditation. An experienced meditator, Ron had developed an unusual facility for cultivating states of deep focus and prolonged concentration. He said he felt peace, rather than sorrow, while experiencing these nonordinary states of unity and bliss. While this immediately translated into a feeling of confidence and a detachment from his stressful emotions, he acknowledged that the underlying issues that contributed to his wife's decision to end their relationship, and his inability to cope with it, remained untouched. The feelings of fragmentation had recently escalated and Ron could no longer escape them by meditating.

Ron grew up in a home in which there was a facade of 'love' without the substance—his parents, both academics and highly preoccupied with their own demanding careers, provided for his physical and educational needs but were detached from his emotional ones. His parents were more comfortable in the realm of logical thought than feelings, and Ron's emotions were rarely engaged and never validated by them. Ron learned at an early age that he would have to take care of himself because his parents were not available for emotional support. Logical thought became a kind of "foster parent," providing a substitute for his emotionally unavailable parents. Ron lived in a realm of pure thought and viewed the world through the prism of his intellect. Emotional conflicts or issues became problems that he strove to solve with logic.

But the onslaught of feelings unleashed by his impending divorce overwhelmed Ron's highly developed capacity for rational thought. One of the benefits he got from meditation was a concrete strategy for attempting to manage his emotional life without the benefit of any other emotional resources. In therapy he eventually realized that meditation anesthetized powerful feelings of loneliness and grief that unwittingly resulted in his avoiding and prolonging the necessary process of mourning and healing.

Spiritual experiences of oneness offered another patient, a depressed woman in her late forties, a way of avoiding the agony of her life. At the beginning of our first session, Eileen immediately launched into a recitation of her spiritual insights with little introduction or hesitation. A highly successful entrepreneur, Eileen nevertheless felt that she was a failure, that life had passed her by. She had no children or husband and was involved in an on-again, off-again relationship with a married man who would never marry her. She renounced normal emotional attachments, claiming that ordinary relationships were unnecessary evils, obstacles to a more important and greater, selfless, spiritual love for humanity. "Real love is unconditional," she informed me, with a coercive tone of voice. "We are one. Fear is a fiction. We are God. If everyone felt the way I feel at this moment there would be peace on earth." Unfortunately there was not much peace in her soul.

Eileen was disconnected from people (colleagues, therapists, friends, and acquaintances) and the world. I was struck by the way her contacts with other people usually devolved into ongoing battles rather than loving friendships. Her belief in and assertion of boundless love and freedom was belied by the acrimony and distance that characterized most of her relationships. But it also enabled her to keep at bay profound and shattering loss: the premature death of both of her parents when she was a young adult, and the regret and disappointment of not getting married or having a child. Feeling connected with the sacred allowed Eileen to believe that her life was not a failure, that it had deep, even transcendental significance. It provided her with an opportunity to feel that she was special and had not missed out on any vital experiences. It was not that she was abandoned and betrayed and might never love or be loved; in her periodic experiences of spiritual "universal consciousness" she experienced the greatest and only really substantial love of all. Eileen had a glimpse of something visionary—the interconnection of people, the power of love, and the holiness of daily life. But since her spiritual experiences were utilized in the service of defensive self-protection they never led to a genuinely self-transformative experience.

In my work with Ron and Eileen I saw the way spiritual experiences can all too often be an unwitting form of pathological mourning, in which traumatic or disturbing experiences of loss, abuse, or neglect in the past are sealed off and the person's current life is endlessly shaped and delimited by these disavowed and unconscious experiences. Mourning is arrested as one enacts rather than remembers, experiences, integrates, and works through one's past.

The spiritual quest, no less than making money or achieving fame, can be recruited to enhance one's stature or self-esteem. Many spiritual aspirants fall victim to what the Tibetan Buddhist teacher Chogyam Trungpa termed "spiritual materialism." I have observed the way one's "spirituality" becomes, for many seekers, a badge of one's specialness in two ways: (1) one's spiritual experiences or attainments lead to self-inflation and (2) what Nietzsche[66] might term one's spiritual asceticism is utilized to make one feel more pious or evolved than those less self-denying. It as if one is saying: "I am better than you because I have less than you."

"It is very remarkable," notes Wittgenstein, "that we should be inclined to think of civilization—houses, trees, cars, etc.—as separating man from his origins, from what is lofty and eternal, etc. Our civilized environment, along with its trees and plants, strikes us then as though cheaply wrapped in cellophane and isolated from everything great, from God, as it were. That is a remarkable picture."[67] Many of us divide the world into the ordinary and The Extraordinary, the secular and The Sacred, the profane and The Holy. We take the first term in each binary opposition for granted, hardly noticing it. We treat the second one with reverence. Once we divide the world into two in this way and then idealize one facet of life and neglect the other part we desanctify ordinary existence. We establish a special realm of experience—that often excludes passion, carnality, afflictive emotions, interpersonal conflicts, and so forth—that is the true and only province of the spiritual. We imagine that this region is beyond or divorced from ordinary, mundane, everyday existence. Getting to this realm or having experiences associated with it ("spiritual" experiences) makes us feel we are part of something larger and elite and justifies our existence. While Zen offers a counterpressure to this—emphasizing the importance of *being-in-the-world,* many spiritual seekers (as Eileen illustrated) are particularly prone to this sort of devaluing of the quotidian world, desanctifying everyday experience. But daily life does deserve our attention and our gratitude. We need to "sanctify the ordinary,"[68] for it is a "treasure and a gift."[69]

The English language and psychoanalytic discourse offer an impoverished vocabulary for evoking non-egocentric states of subjectivity and spiritual experiences. In such experiences of what Kierkegaard, in *Fear and Trembling*, termed "the sublime in the pedestrian,"[70] we are unself-preoccupied yet highly attentive, receptive to the moment but without a sense of time, attuned to otherness but without necessarily being neglectful of the self.[71]

My patients emphasized five aspects of healthy spirituality, as I suggested earlier: an experience of profound unity with the universe, the cultivation of virtuous character, the experience of a pure, uncorrupted sense of self, leading one's life based on deeper meaning and purpose, and the path to any of these experiences. Drawing on Winnicott's view of transitional experiencing, Grotstein's reflections on the transcendent position, Eigen's reflections on spirituality, and my own personal experiences I'll elaborate and extend these reflections.

When you least expect it—walking on a country road, meditating, making love, grappling with a work of art, playing sports—it just happens. You didn't cause it or expect it, although you were open to it. If you were looking for it, it couldn't happen. At least not then. When it happens you are taken by surprise.

When it first happened to me in a basketball game when I was eighteen, I didn't even know it existed. Sometimes it is spawned by pain. Other times silence or beauty. But it is usually unusually intense and compelling. It involves heightened awareness, intensity, and aliveness. You see glory in the flower, grace in the slithering animal in the grass, wonder in the starry skies. Time may elongate. You feel the luminous embedded in the ordinary. You feel centered and balanced, intimate with the universe. You feel the self and the universe are sacred. You are catapulted out of (or into) your self. The sense of yourself expands—at least momentarily—beyond a cohesive, integrated self to a communion and homecoming with the universe. The universe feels more alive and wondrous and less (or non) conflictual. Life has a deeper meaning.

Happiness or peace are bleached-out ways of expressing what you feel. It is Radiant and Luminous. You feel suffused with aliveness. Life being Alive. Spiritual experiences give Life to life. It is good to be alive. Radiant aliveness. Luminous aliveness. Bliss. Aliveness and joy that show you your self is wider and the universe richer than you knew or imagined.[72]

Such spiritual experiences, from my Winnicottian-inspired perspective, are not possessions we have/own or ends to which we strive or even facets of our personalities, but ever-present possibilities of being involving the intersection of self and the larger world.[73] And we must embody spiritual insights in how we live, how we treat ourselves and others. Is our empathy and compassion deepening and expanding? Are we becoming more connected to life? The sacred is all around us. We can experience it in our daily activities, at work, in our homes, and in our relationships, as well as in altered states of consciousness like those I depicted playing basketball. In such moments—that arise in the moment (yet often feel timeless)—there is an intersection of human beings and the world they are embedded in, leading to a sense that there is more than meets the I. In such experiences the individual feels graced by something more, something larger than the self that touches and flows through the self. These moments and experiences represent an opportunity for expanding our sense of identity and overcoming our separateness.

In spiritual experiences one often feels nonseparate from the universe, a sense of oneness with others and the world. This connectedness between self and other is said to lead to a nondualistic outlook that fosters the potential for heightened ethics. Spiritual experiences are often presumed to be connected with the highest morality. Spirituality is often presented, as I suggested earlier, as the antidote to the egocentricity fostered by secular, individualistic culture. Spirituality is claimed to improve our morality and presumed to be essential for psychoanalysis. Symington[74] argues, for example, that psychoanalysis needs religion and spirituality, which contains those core values such as compassion and wisdom that give life meaning. But the issues may sometimes be complex and elusive. Can spiritual experiences ever be amoral?

Experiences of oneness sometimes breed problems as well as open up new worlds. Oneness in the moment can allow some spiritual seekers to avoid ethical responsibility. Zen's emphasis on a wholehearted being-this-moment can lead (although of course it does not always) to immersion in oppressive nationalistic status quos, as was the case with the Samurai's service to whomever was in power. This was quite compatible with World War II Japanese nationalism (Barry Magid, personal communication, 1998).

PSYCHOANALYSIS AND SPIRITUALITY: CLINICAL CONSIDERATIONS

It remains to be considered whether analysis *in itself* must really lead, to the giving up of religion.
                            —Freud to Eitingon, June 20, 1927

In itself psycho-analysis is neither religious nor nonreligious.
                            —Freud to Pfister, February 9, 1909

I suspect that an increasing number of patients, like Joan, seek a life of greater spirituality. Where does this leave the psychoanalyst, who was trained in an analytic culture that valued the clear-eyed reason of science and overwhelmingly pathologized and marginalized religious and spiritual concerns? A moment of Freud's own undogmatic agnosticism about his atheism in *The Future of an Illusion* serves as a suggestive reminder for postclassical psychoanalysts treating people for whom religion and spirituality seem to be of increasing concern. "If experience should show—not to me—but to others after me, who think the same way—that we have been mistaken" [in our critique of religion] writes Freud, "then we will renounce our expectations."[75] Traditionally, the spiritual path and psychoanalysis have been segregated. Then spiritual teachers and seekers all too readily assume that the spiritual path uniquely possesses the truth about human experience. Psychotherapeutic disciplines are devalued and neglected. There needs to be a rapprochement of psychoanalysis and spirituality in which they each are more receptive to what light the other might shed on the art of living. A *contemplative psychoanalysis* would appreciate the constructive as well as the pathological facets of spiritual experiences. If it is antianalytic to treat spiritual experiences as inherently psychopathological, as the majority of psychoanalysts have done, it is unanalytic to take spiritual claims at face value, without inquiring into the complex and multidimensional meanings and functions they uniquely possess in the mind and heart of a particular person in psychoanalytic treatment. There needs to be a close encounter of a new kind between psychoanalysis and the spiritual quest, in which neither discipline is presumed to have unique access to the sovereign truth and they are neither seg-regated from each other nor assimilated into one another. Psychoanalytic impe-rialism emerges when it tries to conquer spiritual experiences; when it has a "nothing but" attitude toward them; when everything spiritual is explained by and reduced to psychoanalytic categories. But spiritual traditions need to avoid their own brand of intellectual (or spiritual) imperialism in which a spiritual text or meditational practice is treated as if it is the final truth about reality. Psy-choanalysis and the spiritual quest have different, although at times overlapping, concerns. If they are too separate and autonomous, then fruitful contact is pre-cluded. No meaningful cross-pollination is possible when they are segregated and isolated. If they are too merged, then important differences are eclipsed. The task for psychoanalysis and spiritual disciplines, like the challenge for indi-viduals in a committed relationship, is to balance autonomy and connected-ness[76] so that there is intimacy that preserves and enriches the autonomy of each.

What are the clinical consequences of my perspective on spirituality and psychoanalysis? Therapists rarely talk about their spiritual life and its impact on treatment. There are sound and time-tested reasons for this, ranging from not wishing to shape the transference to not wanting to infringe on the patient's autonomy. The dearth of discussions of spirituality and psychoanalytic treat-ment seems to make it a taboo topic in psychoanalysis. But then the impact of an analyst's spiritual views and spiritual life—including his or her atheism—is rendered unconscious. In the spirit of bringing to consciousness something that could enrich psychoanalysis I will offer some very tentative reflections on this subject. My remarks are provisional speculations, rather than fully formed conclusions.

Spirituality affects my theory and practice of therapy in explicit and implicit ways. While it is rarely a topic of discussion—only when it is brought up by the patient—it has an indirect impact in ways that I can only sometimes articulate. I will artificially divide my remarks into theoretical and clinical con-siderations. I realize the lines between them are, in practice, more blurry.

My spiritual experiences have influenced my view of the world as well as my conception of human nature and human relationships. This affects how I think of the therapeutic relationship and the possibilities of treatment to gener-ate change. Ever since I had the spiritual experience I mentioned toward the beginning of this chapter I have understood the truth of the French surrealist poet Paul Eluard's remark that "there is another world and it is in this one." There is more to life than is dreamt of in our psychoanalytic psychologies. While psychoanalysis is skilled at exploring and revealing the fallaciousness of vacuous and illusory hopes, there is a mirror-opposite danger in psychoanalysis that, like Freud, we will normalize and universalize a tragic and melancholic view of the universe. I see life as a dialogic movement of change and stasis with personal evolution an ever-present possibility. Patients have, I believe, definite biological, existential, and psychological constraints. But they also have undreamt of creative potentials. This gives me more hope than I might have if I subscribed to the kind of tragic view of the universe that permeates psychoanalysis.

Psychoanalysis lacks compelling visions of the self after analysis, as Bollas[77] notes. Spiritual experiences have convinced me that psychoanalytic conceptions of health are too limited and dispirited. There is more to life than achieving common human unhappiness or the depressive position. Having spiritual experiences gives me a different—I believe fuller—sense of human possibilities. There may be capacities for empathy and compassion that psychoanalysis has not yet mapped. A story about Gandhi is illustrative. A man attended one of Gandhi's spiritual talks with the goal of assassinating him. But he was so moved by the power of Gandhi's teachings that he scrapped his plan. After Gandhi spoke, the assassin prostrated himself in front of Gandhi and tearfully informed him that he had been hired to kill him but that after hearing him he no longer could carry out his original plan. Imagine for a second that someone told you that they had planned to kill you and then knelt in front of you. How would you feel? Gandhi looked the assassin in the eyes with deep compassion and said: "How are you going to explain to the people who hired you about your failure to carry out the plan?" Gandhi empathized with the plight of his nemesis even when his own life had been threatened.

"It is impossible to escape the impression," notes Freud in the opening sentence of *Civilization and Its Discontents*, "that people commonly use false standards of measurement—that they seek power, success and wealth for themselves and admire them in others, and that they underestimate what is of true value in life." Although spiritual traditions each have their own world view, beliefs, and practices, they tend, in general, like Freud, to critique conventional societal values. Not only do they challenge the egocentricity and materialism of secular worldviews, they also tend to offer an alternative system of values based on selflessness, compassion, altruism, and wisdom. My values have been affected by the spiritual experiences that I have had. Many people in our culture—even those who scoff at the vacuousness of conspicuous consumption—live as if wealth directly correlates with happiness. But expanded material comforts in the twenty-first century have not necessarily deepened our individual or collective peace of mind. Although there is no inherent virtue in poverty and financial struggles obviously do not foster inner peace and contentment, economic prosperity does not resolve our fundamental psychological and spiritual questions or problems. What I have observed clinically—partially as a result of already believing it and thus looking for it—is that people often suffer because of the search for fame and material goods as well as because of the panoply of causes that psychoanalysts have so ably elucidated. My spiritual background has led me to question patients' values such as consumerism—especially the correlation between wealth and happiness. My spiritual experiences have led to a less dualistic view of the relationship between people, by which I mean that I see self and other as deeply connected and irreducibly interrelated. I have a deep and abiding sense that patient and analyst are not-two, and that we are both in the treatment together. While I am not responsible for their life, their choices, even for how they use the treatment, I feel a deep commitment to fully engaging the process.

The second crucial way that spiritual experiences shape my work is non-specific and personal; it affects who I *am* in the treatment—my *being*, that is, the quality of my presence in the room. I have periodically been told by certain patients that something healing is transmitted in the treatment—especially a quality of deep attentiveness, nonjudgmentalness, and serenity. A story from the Zen tradition points toward the attentiveness I am referring to. A Zen student goes to his teacher. The student is very excited about his spiritual accomplishments and can hardly contain himself as he waits to tell his teacher. It is raining on the day that he visits. He takes off his shoes and puts his umbrella down outside his teacher's room. He enters the room and launches into a recitation about the insights he has had meditating. The master says to him: "It is raining today, did you bring an umbrella?"

"Yes I brought an umbrella," the student says. "But let me tell you what I experienced in my meditation."

"On which side of your shoes did you put the umbrella?" the teacher asks.

"I have no idea," the student says, as he prepares to relate the extraordinary experiences he had meditating.

"Go and practice more moment-by-moment Zen," the teacher advises him. Immersion in meditation practice for over two decades has heightened my attentiveness in the treatment, including my receptivity to my countertransference and creative imagination and intuition.

Spiritual experiences have fostered in me a deeper sense of the mystery of the universe and human development and treatment. This has encouraged more receptivity to the unknown in therapy. Aware of the *more* than what I currently know and believe, I am more able and willing to surrender to the therapeutic process and let go of beliefs of how treatment should unfold. I feel that my patients are potential supervisors, as Langs and Searles[78] have so ably written about, which breeds, I suspect, a less defensive attitude about my theories or the correctness of my insights or interpretations. It makes me hold my theories lightly rather than tightly.

Hope, connectedness, and nondefensiveness may create a different kind of intersubjective space between me and the patient—one that is infused with safety, curiosity, openness, and respect. Therapy is then a "sacred space" in which shame may be decreased and greater openness is fostered. Patients are encouraged to say and experience what they had not been able to utter before, and to be heard in ways that they didn't expect and had not previously known.

SPIRITUALITY AND WHOLENESS

In this chapter I have attempted to depict what spirituality is; why it is important to our current cultural moment, how it might enrich psychoanalysis, and how psychoanalytic understandings might aid spiritual seekers in avoiding a variety of potential pitfalls.

Spirituality plays an incredibly vital role in our culture, as I suggested earlier, expanding and enriching human subjectivity; connecting us to a larger reality in which we are all embedded; reenchanting the world; disclosing undreamt of dimensions of being; and infusing our lives with mystery and vitality, awe and wonder. A world without spirit is impoverished. Life without a purpose larger than individual fulfillment is alienating and has no meaning. Narcissism reigns. Value and wonder are eclipsed. A universe that values spiritual experiences can be deeply enriched.

The repression of spirituality in psychoanalysis and the culture at large contributes to the enormous alienation, anomie, and melancholy that permeate the lives of many people. Psychoanalysis, like the larger culture it is embedded in, suffers because it only intermittently realizes that there is more than meets the I. Fullness or wholeness of being necessitates an openness to and an experiencing of broader dimensions of life that can be revealed, as they were to me, in spiritual experiences.

Psychoanalysis could benefit from retrieving spiritual experiences split off in the modern age when the self became separate and isolated. Spiritual experiences extend relational thinking, suggesting that it is not simply the self-in-relation-to-a-caregiving-(or therapeutic) matrix, but a self-in-relation-to-a-larger-life-world.

But the notion of spirituality has become in our culture what the literary critic Kenneth Burke[79] termed, a "god-term," a universal category beyond examination. It is central to our existence, but it also seems the site of numerous illusions and abuses.

Psychoanalysis is traditionally viewed as an atheistic science of human subjectivity or, more recently, intersubjectivity. The atheism is often taken for granted and unconscious. It is a kind of silent backdrop, part of an invisible and unacknowledged assumptive framework for viewing the world and conducting psychoanalytic treatment. It tends only to emerge when religiously committed patients are in treatment. It then generates a great deal of countertransference, as many analysts view religion and spiritual experiences through the distorting lens of knee-jerk pathologizing.

But psychoanalysis can also appreciate spiritual experience without the mystifications of organized religion. Psychoanalysis offers tools, as I suggested earlier, to elucidate pathologies and pitfalls on the spiritual path. If contemplative traditions temper the egocentricity of psychoanalytic accounts of self-experience and thereby deabsolutize the self-centered self, then psychoanalytic attention to psychological complexity and the shaping role of unconsciousness in human thought and action might deprovincialize the non self-centered, contemplative self.[80]

There is no guarantee that blissful absorptive union leads to intimacy, self-understanding, or moral action. Fusion experiences are no guarantee of goodness, as survivors of sexual abuse know all too well. Since spirituality can sometimes lead to self-evasion or even immorality it needs to be integrated with psychological wisdom and moral sensitivity.

Spirituality lives in the everyday, where there is no separation or segregation between the sacred and the profane; where the profane (including otherness and self-care, imminence as well as transcendence, carnality no less than compassion) is sacred and the sacred is profane. Spiritual seekers often desacrilize and devalue ordinary existence when they separate and segregate the sacred and the profane. Passion, intimacy, and carnality can get eclipsed. Because of its attention to the moment and to mundane and embodied existence, as opposed to otherworldly disembodied transcendence, psychoanalysis can sacrilize the ordinary, reveal the imminence of the divine, and foster this-worldly spirituality and morality.

Karl Marx revealed our social unconscious. Sigmund Freud illuminated our personal unconscious. I wonder if in the twenty-first century we need to become aware of the "sacred unconscious."[81] If we get in touch with the personal unconscious, we are less driven and imprisoned by the past. We are more liberated from the demons that have haunted us. If we perceive the social unconscious, we are aware of social conditioning and exploitation and we are more individuated from our culture and its values. If we appreciate the sacred unconscious, we would see the world as more holy; we would see it whole. The world would be experienced as more magical and enchanted. We would celebrate life in all its inexhaustible vibrancy and diversity. We would feel more serenity and joy. There would be less distance between people and we would feel more compassion toward nature and other beings.

Psychoanalysis at its best can demystify spiritual abuses without eclipsing the possibility of spiritual experiences. A nonreductionistic *contemplative psychoanalysis* of the future, in which spiritual experiences were valued as well as critically examined, could foster a civilization with greater meaning and sacredness and less discontent.[82]

CHAPTER FIVE

PSYCHOANALYSIS
AND THE GOOD LIFE

To live! To live! So natural and so hard.
—James Schuyler

IN THE COURSE OF EXPLORING HIS FEAR OF DEATH, a patient, a man in his mid thirties, said that what he actually feared was "not really living." As we examined what he meant by "not really living," he began speaking about "living a full life." The quest to live a good life has a venerable history. The central concern for Lao Tzu, Buddha, Socrates, Aristotle, Epicurus, Jesus, the Prophets, Montaigne, Thoreau, Nietzsche, Marx, and Schweitzer, among others—those individuals Fromm calls "masters of living"[1]—was how humans should live. Two ways of thinking about this broad and important topic dominate contemporary thinking: a secular, materialistic ideal and a spiritual one.

François Rabelais ends his satirical masterpiece *Gargantua* with the construction of the Abbey of Thélème. In Thélème wealth, happiness, and pleasure are the goals of life. In our world the good life is often linked to similar hedonistic images. The "good life," or full life, conjures up a variety of associations, including "having it all": the unlimited freedom to purchase and accumulate; the ability to obtain ceaseless pleasure, luxury, and ease; and the power to shape one's life and segregate oneself from noxious external impingements, including any unwanted obligations and constraints. The media—movies, television, books, magazines, and newspapers—exalt this kind of life. A large percentage of people in our society find this goal enormously compelling and judge themselves according to whether they actually embody this ideal. Believing, with

87

AT&T, that "it's all within your reach," the unconscious (sometimes conscious) assumption for the vast majority of people is that if they achieve this goal, then they will be happy.

That there is not a direct correlation between wealth and emotional health is probably not news to any analyst who has listened to the disillusionment and sometimes despair of their financially wealthier patients. Obviously even the very affluent experience a great deal of alienation and emptiness and the feeling that "there has to be something more." "Having it all" does not necessarily constitute a life well-lived and in fact is sometimes an obstacle to it. This is not surprising. The most remarkable feature of the Abbey of Thélème, after all, is its thick walls, not its hedonism and sensuous delight. From inside one has privacy and is secluded from the outside world. But one also cannot see the other side. Good fences, claims Robert Frost, make good neighbors. They also make good prisons. The wall at Thélème fences its inhabitants in as well as keeps outsiders out.

There is a countervailing perspective on the good life that is increasingly popular in our world—namely, the "spiritual" point of view. Spiritual perspectives on the good life in our culture offer a powerful counterpressure to the ceaseless pursuit of wealth and leisure. Although they do not offer a monolithic formula they do seem to share several compatible features such as the attempt to discover and embody our essential, authentic self, the idealization of selflessness, and the belief in an uncontaminated realm that it is humanly possible to experience permanently "beyond ego." Pursuing the "soul's code"—as if it is a singular essence—is presumed to lead to living authentically and purely. Living life for others is assumed to eradicate egocentricity and promote balanced and sane living.

There are a growing number of people who find this view compelling. But the rash of scandals in spiritual communities in recent years involving supposedly selfless and self-realized teachers displaying rampant egocentricity and complete lack of moral accountability cast grave doubt on spiritual images of the good life and the ideal of selflessness.

Psychoanalysis complicates secular and spiritual pictures of the well-lived life by critiquing the apsychological moralities of Buddhism and other contemplative traditions, which simplify psychological life and ethics. Psychoanalysis demonstrates how the accounts of the good life in these traditions neglect the ubiquity of self-deception and the shaping role of the past—the way our individual and family histories close down as well as open up certain possibilities. Experiences in childhood determine and restrict how well we care for ourselves and relate to others and the world. The stubbornness of character, transference, and unconsciousness is also neglected in these traditions.[2] Contemplative traditions pay insufficient attention to the way intentions and actions may have multiple unconscious meanings and functions. Altruism in a spiritual practitioner may hide vanity and piousness. Self-denigration may masquerade as spiritual asceticism. Humility can be fueled by a sense of non-entitlement or fear of competition no less than a recognition of the suffering and limitation generated by an excessively possessive relation to a theory, object, or practice.

The problems with both contemplative and secular conceptions of a life well-lived leave us adrift, lacking a guiding vision or a framework for action. It is a central claim of this chapter that psychoanalysis might be an unexpected resource in this area, making a significant contribution to this topic.

I began this chapter after receiving an invitation by a colleague, George Silbershatz, to participate in a psychoanalytic symposium on "Psychoanalysis and Suffering." Aware of my writings on psychoanalysis and contemplative traditions,[3] particularly Buddhist psychology, he hoped that I would bring a perspective on human suffering gleaned from Buddhism. I was eager to participate in such a dialogue, but as I thought about the topic I was troubled as well as intrigued. As I became curious about what disturbed me, I realized that the topic seemed symptomatic of something that bothered me about psychoanalysis—namely, its overemphasis on what afflicts us and its neglect of what nourishes, sustains, and vitalizes us. To speak of suffering without speaking of the Good Life could reenact psychoanalysis's imbalanced view of life, which itself could contribute to suffering. I was intrigued with the topic because I hoped that reflecting on this lacuna in psychoanalysis might lead to something edifying.

Psychoanalysis seems, at first glance, ill-equipped for elucidating the good life because of its tragic worldview (with its focus on illness, not health), its concentration on the isolated unencumbered individual, and its commitment to moral neutrality.

Psychoanalysis is underwritten by a "tragic" worldview—that is, a recognition of the inescapable mysteries, dilemmas, and afflictions pervading human existence.[4] Tragic does not necessarily imply, contrary to popular usage, "unhappy or disastrous outcomes,"[5] but rather a steadfast recognition that time is irreversible and unredeemable; humans are beings moving toward death, not rebirth; choices entail conflict and compromise; and suffering is inevitable. Religious consolations are quixotic in the tragic vision.[6] Deriving from and intimately connected to its tragic worldview, psychoanalysis is a psychology of illness that neglects health, creativity, intimacy, and spirituality. Because psychoanalysis has focused on pathology it tends to conceive of health, as Freud's "pathography" of Leonardo illustrates, as an absence of illness rather than the presence of well-being. Psychoanalysis, as Winnicott aptly noted, has "yet to tackle the question of what *life itself is about*" apart from illness.[7] There are, of course, certain exceptions such as Rank, Ferenczi, Jung, Fromm, Milner, Eigen, and Grotstein, to highlight some key figures.

Contemplative perspectives on the human condition suggest that psychoanalysis contributes to suffering by its tragic and secular worldview and by systematically underestimating human possibilities for healing and health. It is thus

not surprising that the concept of the good life rarely appears in the psychoanalytic literature. To read psychoanalytic accounts of the "ends of analysis"—personal integration, heightened reality testing, the capacity to "love and work,"
developing ego strength, and cultivating the ability for self-reflection and self-
analysis—is to understand why artists and spiritual seekers, among others, all
too often believe that there is more on earth (I don't know about heaven) than
psychoanalytic accounts of the good life suggest.

Given psychoanalysis's avowed commitment to moral neutrality, it may
sound strange at first to speak of psychoanalysis and the good life. The good life
or the full life is not something that psychoanalysis usually is or should be prescriptive about. One of the many virtues of psychoanalysis is that, unlike
ancient spiritual traditions or contemporary psychospiritual writings, it does
not legislate or provide formulaic answers to the Socratic question of how one
should live one's life. There are many virtues to such an attitude, including the
minimization of coercive external impositions, the protection of the patient's
autonomy, and the openness to many different ways of living.

Given the neglect of health in psychoanalysis and the reluctance to engage
values, pychoanalysis seems like an unpromising candidate for illuminating the
well-lived life. In fact, psychoanalysis may not seem to offer anything to this
topic unless we approach it psychoanalytically, by which I mean reading psychoanalysis against its grain, questioning standard interpretations (even psychoanalytic ones), searching for hidden as opposed to manifest meanings and
implications in psychoanalytic formulations, and treating what is not said by
psychoanalysts as sometimes as meaningful as what is said. To take up a
"Freudian" attitude toward psychoanalysis itself is to be interested in unconscious facets of psychoanalytic reflections. Since the full implications of analytic
views of the good life are only germinally present in analytic writings, the
legacy about the good life may only be partially evident until it is explicitly
fleshed out and articulated. Many people assume that the good life, for Freud,
involves the capacity to approach life with clear-eyed rationality, to peel away
distorting illusions including unrealistic religious hopes for salvation, to bear
life's burdens with greater clarity and stoical equanimity, and to love and work
with a measure of success and fulfillment. But there are additional implications
about a life well-lived in the writings of Freud and his successors, and uses to
which psychoanalytic perspectives can be put that analysts may not always have
consciously intended and of which they may not always be fully aware.

It is often assumed outside psychoanalysis—occasionally even within it—
that psychoanalysis is normalizing, by which I mean that it is a form of social
control and conformity. But psychoanalysis is transgressive and denormalizing
as well as domesticating. Psychoanalysis illustrates its liberatory potential when
it challenges and extends the normative standards that it elsewhere establishes.
More fertile and suggestive perspectives on the good life emerge when psy-

choanalysis questions and destabilizes its own authority rather than when it establishes universalistic models.

Although psychoanalysis has usefully eschewed a prescriptive perspective on values, implicit in psychoanalysis are a variety of suggestive perspectives on a life well-lived. Despite the commitment to helping patients find their own answers to questions about how to live, psychoanalysis is not, nor could it ever be, neutral about such topics, as I suggested in chapter two. Embedded in psychoanalysis are all sorts of conscious and unconscious notions about the kinds of values and lives that are worth living. In this chapter I will attempt to explore and make more conscious what W. H. Auden termed "the dreams of Eden,"[8] the visions of the good life that psychoanalysis values. Rendering them more conscious opens up tacit knowledge encoded within psychoanalysis that may remain buried and thus not accessible for enriching us if it remains undetected. Explicitly delineating psychoanalytic visions of the good life also gives us the opportunity to be more reflective about these conceptions, which could contribute to living a fuller life.

Illuminating the nature of the good life is important for psychoanalysis for at least two reasons: the first is clinical, the second cultural. Psychoanalysis is not value-neutral. The analyst has a vision of the good life even if he or she does not consciously formulate it and consciously subscribes to the view that an analyst should have no vision apart from that of neutrally applying the analytic method. To know when to terminate a treatment, the analyst must have an image of cure; to know what a cure is, one must have a vision of the good life. These visions shape our daily work in hidden ways that are no less important because they are unconscious. In fact, they are more formative because they are hidden.

The second reason the topic of the good life is important has to do with psychoanalysis's problematic standing in and relation to the contemporary world. We live in two senses in a demoralized world. Many people feel discouraged, beaten down, and defeated. Second, we are in an age in which morality is the exception, where hedonism reigns in most domains of human conduct. Elected officials, religious figures, executives, entertainers, and professional athletes do what enhances the self and are without scruples or concern for their impact on others. In a world that resembles a moral free-for-all—where anything goes—people are left with no foundations or guiding direction for action. As a consequence, many individuals are adrift. What fills the breach is egocentricity, hedonism, popular psychospiritual quick fixes, and addictive behavior. Is it surprising that we feel moral malaise?

Psychoanalysis is in a good position to illuminate the good life for at least three reasons:

1. Psychoanalysis is a sanctuary from the cognitive oversaturation, emotional disconnection, and pressure to live flattened lives that

permeate our culture.[9] This provides an emotionally intimate, and relatively non-impinging context for exploring such questions of ultimate concern as how one should live.

2. Psychoanalysis is in a position to illuminate the good life because it has access to depths of human subjectivity that are not explored anywhere else in daily life. Psychoanalysis appreciates unconsciousness, which religious and spiritual disciplines all too often neglect. It also is a "hermeneutics of suspicion"—challenging and attempting to demystify taken-for-granted motives and meanings.[10]

3. Psychoanalysis, unlike postmodernistic discourse, is critical yet *reconstuctive,* demystifying and *affirmative.* Psychoanalysts question the authority humans often irrationally invest in others, yet they do not deny expertise. Psychoanalysts recognize that there is no objectivity, but they do not usher in a disabling nihilism. Psychoanalysts drain the bath water of self-mastery without throwing out the baby of self-complexity.

And yet, despite psychoanalysis's potential to illuminate the Good Life, one could search in vain for psychoanalytic citations on this topic. There are no references to it, for example, in the *Standard Edition* of Freud. Erich Fromm[11] and Leslie Farber[12] are in a distinct minority in addressing this important and neglected topic. There are at least four reasons why this topic has been neglected in psychoanalysis.

1. Hitching its star to science was one important way that psychoanalysis tried to legitimate itself in a psychoanalytically inhospitable world. Neutrality was central to the self-image of science. The legacy of neutrality made analysts queasy about the anxiety of influence. It is thus normal analytic practice for the analyst to refrain from expressing any ideas about the Good Life to the patient.

2. Novick[13] has comprehensively illuminated psychoanalysts' resistance to termination and the terminal phase of treatment. Since it is in this phase of treatment that reflections on cure and the good life may explicitly play the most central role, neglecting termination meant that the issue of health was slighted by psychoanalysts.

3. The fully analyzed patient (or analyst) is more readily viewed as a fiction in contemporary psychoanalysis. Recognizing the illusoriness of perfectionistic ideals of a "complete analysis," we analysts may neglect the topic of health.

4. With its tragic worldview, psychoanalysis is a psychology of illness, focusing on what goes wrong in development. Is it any wonder that analysts, to borrow from Shakespeare, "know what we are but

not what we may be." Psychoanalysis tends to debunk what is positive in the search for the hidden and seamy underside of apparently constructive ideals and behavior.

PSYCHOANALYTIC VIEWS OF THE GOOD LIFE

The examined life is, for Freud, essential to the good life. Freud continued and radically extended the centuries-old Augustinian tradition of depthful self-investigation with his writings on the unconscious, transference, resistance, and dreamwork. Since Freud plumbed the unconscious, human reflection, action, and morality have been greatly complicated. The unconscious is another word for the ubiquity of self-deception, the impossibility of unmediated and uncontaminated self-awareness, and the possibility of exquisite creativeness. We are not transparent to ourselves. Actions and intentions have multiple conscious and unconscious meanings and functions. There are at least four morals to this story: In such a world, (1) we have an endless capacity to deceive ourselves; (2) we can never completely know ourselves; (3) we have an enormous potential for unconsciously communicating with ourselves and healing ourselves, and (4) the examined life is never-ending.

Once self-transparency is seen as an illusion, then the examined life is regarded as unceasing. Sainthood and enlightenment are viewed in a different, more Orwellian light. "[S]ainthood is also a thing that human beings must avoid," claims Orwell.[14] "The essence of being human," according to Orwell, "is that one does not seek perfection, that one *is* sometimes willing to commit sins for the sake of loyalty, that one does not push asceticism to the point where it makes friendly intercourse impossible, and that one is prepared in the end to be defeated and broken up by life, which is the inevitable price of fastening one's love upon other human beings."[15]

The pessimism and stoicism that commentators have correctly pinpointed in Freud emerge, in part, out of this kind of sensibility. In Japanese aesthetics there is a great emphasis on "*wabi sabi*," sometimes translated as the "beauty" of things "imperfect" and "incomplete."[16] A deep strand of Platonic idealism permeates ordinary conceptions of justice, ethics, and health, by which I mean that many people believe there is an essential essence called 'justice' or 'truth' or 'health.' It serves as an ideal to which those individuals aspire. But the record of human history reveals the opposite; the pervasiveness of injustice, dishonesty, and illness. Eschewing the illusory ideals of perfection that permeate our culture, psychoanalysis joins Orwell and Japanese aesthetics in a *this*-worldly conception of living, which provides a realistic ideal as well as tempers the quick-fix mentality that reigns in our culture.

But psychoanalysis offers more. There is a counterpressure in Freud's work on childhood, the unconscious, and dreamwork. There is a deep human predilection to reduce, to narrow down. "Newton's vision and single sleep," Blake termed it. We search for our essence, speculate about our destiny. It is reassuring. It creates an apparent order—a world that can be mapped. In the words of Emily Dickinson: "The Soul selects her own society/Then shuts the door/On her divine majority/Obtrude no more . . . I've known her from an ample nation/Choose one/Then close the valves of her attention."[17] The nature of dreamwork—particularly its idiosyncratic meaning and nature—suggests, as I claimed in chapter one, that we are all—even the most prosaic among us—potential artists, capable of creating fertile, unique, and often surreal dreamscapes that capture with brilliant lucidity and specificity our hopes and fears.

"Seekers after truth," e. e. cummings cautions, "follow no path/all paths lead where/truth is here."[18] Psychoanalysis is the art of the idiographic. The notion of the unconscious and dream mentation suggests that the good life is unique rather than standard brand, customized rather than Procrustean.

From Buddhism to behaviorism, our culture is permeated with the implicit as well as explicit search to transcend the dizzying complexity of inner life and embodied existence. Melanie Klein[19] pointed to the irreducibly fluid nature of mental life, the way we experience alternating states of being each with its own particular styles of relatedness and defensiveness. Mental health, for Klein, is a process, not a destination. It involves skillfully navigating the ever-changing and sometimes turbulent waters of our lives rather than reaching a static, preordained final state of being. The implication is that the good life entails engaging and embracing life moment-to-moment in its messiness and complexity rather than striving for a permanent and irreversible developmental milestone or endpoint,[20] which is ultimately quixotic.

For Ferenczi it was possible not only to experience mental health, but to lead a more unfettered life. In his reflections on dissolving transference and super-ego formations and living elastically, there are intimations of the liberatory psychoanalysis he was pursuing:

> it is the business of a real character analysis to do away, at any rate temporarily, with any kind of super-ego, including that of the analyst. The patient should end by ridding himself of any emotional attachment that is independent of his own reason and his own libidinal tendencies. Only a complete dissolution of the super-ego can bring about a radical cure. Successes that consist in the substitution of one super-ego for another must be regarded as transference successes; they fail to attain the final aim of therapy, the dissolution of the transference. . . . The ideal result of a completed analysis is precisely that elasticity which analytic technique demands of the mental therapist.[21]

Freud taught us that the past often betrays the present, making us see ourselves and others in the present in old and restrictive ways. In Ferenczi's provocative vision of the good life we could shed a past that deforms our present so that we could lead an uncoerced and unfettered life, a life in which our past doesn't impinge on and distort our life in the present. We don't free-associate in order to be cured, claims Ferenczi, as I mentioned in the previous chapter; we are cured when we can free-associate,[22] by which I think he meant living with greater playfulness, freedom, authenticity, and spontaneity rather than social conformity, automatic compliance, or self-neglectful responsibility for others.

In Jung's vision, the field of what constitutes the well-lived life expands. For Jung, individuation (becoming our uniqueness), wholeness (integrating opposites within ourselves—including male and female qualities and values—and developing our full humanity), and living with a "religious attitude" (an attitude of being embedded in a larger life-world imbued with depth, sacredness, and meaning) are central to living the good life. The Jungian emphasis on the integration of opposites is very important because of what the Greeks and the Stoics termed the "mutual entailment of the virtues" (*antakolouthia*).[23] We ordinarily think of virtues as self-sufficient, complete, and, as it were, capable of standing on their own. But no virtue or quality—even apparently exalted ones such as honesty or awareness—is virtuous by itself. Authentic virtue requires the balancing and integration of seeming opposites. Honesty without compassion, for example, is cruelty. Awareness devoid of action remains merely intellectual knowledge.

Two traditions dominate the quest to live a moral life, according to Rorty: the ascetic life of self-purification urged by Plato and criticized by Nietzsche and the aesthetic life of "self-enlargement" criticized by Kierkegaard, "the desire to embrace more and more possibilities, to be constantly learning, to give oneself over entirely to curiosity."[24] Such a life is devoted to self-creation and "seeks to extend its own bounds."[25] Psychoanalysis, as Rorty notes, "opened up new possibilities for the aesthetic life."[26]

There is a psychoanalytic "fall." For analysts such as Winnicott, Loewald, and Phillips, the process of growing up and being acculturated into adulthood erodes the curiosity, passion, sensuousness, and aliveness of the child. As children adapt to language, social groups, and cultural and familial norms and expectations, they lose much of the vitality of their childhood.

An ethos of asceticism and an accompanying melancholia pervade psychoanalysis. Psychoanalysis, not unlike Epictetus, Marcus Aurelius, and the Montaigne of "Experience," partakes of a tradition of humane pessimism. A strong renunciate spirit permeates psychoanalysis. Most people in daily life attempt to get what they want. But psychoanalysis since Freud, tacitly or explicitly, counsels renouncing, foregoing, or abstaining from unrealistic or illusory desires and wishes. If "appetite lost" is an implicit facet of the classical psychoanalytic vision of the Good Life, then "appetite regained"[27] is crucial to what I would provisionally term the "aestheticist" wing of postclassical psychoanalysis. The artist, with his or her creativity, authenticity, spontaneity, and aliveness, embodied for

Winnicott, as it did years before for Otto Rank, the Good Life from this vantage point. The Good Life, for contemporary analysts along this axis, such as Loewald, Phillips, and Eigen, involves curiosity and exuberance, aliveness and vibrancy, passion and ecstasy.[28]

Psychoanalysis is reconstructive as well as deconstructive. Like postmodern thought, it can and does reveal the impoverishment of certain idols. But while postmodernistic discourse usually leaves us adrift after usefully questioning established meanings and motives and unraveling taken-for-granted axioms, psychoanalysis makes affirmation no less than negation crucial. One can, that is, question and affirm, even as one deconstructs and undermines. Psychoanalysis's *post*postmodernist perspective, what I have termed its *posthumanism,* offers a unique perspective on self and freedom, among other topics. Psychospiritual writings herald the finding of an authentic, idealized, essential, selfless self. In the emphasis on the idealized, singular self, they provide a more exalted, spiritual, and selfless vision than contemporary culture. "You be you," Nike commercials beseech us. "Be all that you can be," ads for the army implore us. But are we singular? And do we have a particular destiny? Postmodern discourse recognizes our complexity, but then claims that our existence is illusory—a Lacanian mirage. Displaying the complexity and fluidity of self-experience, contemporary relationists such as Stolorow, Atwood, Hoffman, Eigen, Bromberg, and Mitchell, among others, suggest that it is possible to recognize our multidimensionality without jettisoning our individuality/singularity. They also make us more skeptical about the singular, essentialistic, and authentic self of contemplative and pop psychospiritual writings. A richer sense of human subjectivity is then possible.[29]

People demand it and forfeit it, seek it and lose it. What is this ideal we call freedom? Freedom, as John Maynard Keyes, somewhere said, demands eternal vigilance. The examined life is interminable. Freedom is often talked about in contemporary popular and academic discourse in polarized terms; we are free or we are determined; we are puppets of language and history or we are capable of just saying no, just doing it. The work of Freud in particular and psychoanalysis in general suggests that the terms of these debates are problematic because they polarize what are mutually interconnected and reinforcing experiences of being: namely, being determined and having the capacity for reflection and self-transformation. The unconscious reveals the impossibility of self-mastery and self-transcendence. Although we are all authors of our own lives, our authorship is not without constraints. We are also determined. Freedom for Freud was always contextual and relative, never absolute; what in the yogic tradition is a freedom-within-structure, or what Peter Gay in a felicitous phrase termed Freud's "deterministic psychology of freedom."[30] One could never transcend what Shakespeare termed "the ten thousand shocks that flesh is heir to" from this perspective, but one could gain a measure of freedom.

With freedom comes responsibility. Again contemporary popular and academic discussions tend to establish false contrasts, dichotomizing and segregating empathy and moral duty. Right-wing political commentators demand moral accountability, but neglect empathy for the downtrodden or oppressed. Those who evince empathy for the downtrodden all too often jettison ethical accountability. At its best, psychoanalysis encourages empathic understanding of the experience of the oppressed or evildoer while also acknowledging moral responsibility. Moral responsibility, for psychoanalysts such as Hans Loewald,[31] involves integrating and drawing on our histories rather than being excessively detached from or driven by them. While the psychoanalytic emphasis on the wishes and needs of the lone individual can certainly feed the culture of egoistic individualism, it can also serve as an invaluable resource for helping persons to delineate and work through prejudices and negative projections onto and scapegoating of the other, as well as take on "moral responsibilities, including public ones, that they have shunned out of neurotic anxiety."[32]

Morality involves how we treat others. Contemporary relational psychoanalysis demonstrates our irreducibly relational nature. The Good Life, for interpersonally oriented authors such as Levenson, entails working through the interpersonal mystifications created by parents (and sometimes inadvertently one's analyst) and developing interpersonal sensitivity, competence, and know-how, as well as personal fulfillment. Other contemporary interpersonalists such as Bromberg and Mitchell link the good life to self-complexity and relational efficacy, enriching one's internal object world and interpersonal relations.[33]

Love is also central to the good life, as I have discussed in chapter three. Psychoanalysis has neglected and provided an impoverished account of love,[34] which heightens the importance of Fromm and Kohut for alternative perspectives on the Good Life. The Good Life for psychoanalytic existentialists such as Fromm involves authenticity and self-realization, creativity and concern, compassion and interpersonal intimacy.[35] Along these lines, Kohut stressed the role of empathy and attunement to the other. We are always and inevitably connected to others. The Good Life, according to Kohut, involves relationships that are empathic, mutually respectful, affirming, and enriching. He also emphasized living with greater self-coherence, wisdom, humor, and awareness of transience.[36]

Psychoanalysis does not provide a single account of the Good Life. I have highlighted several key dimensions of a life well-lived ranging from self-awareness to interpersonal attunement. What are some of the morals of the tales psychoanalysis tells about a well-lived life? Psychoanalysis suggests that the Good Life is protean rather than standard brand. There is no single best way of living. The patient must discover and create how she wants to live rather than accommodate to anyone else's version, including the analyst's. Since inner experience is fluid rather than static, this changes moment to moment. Health involves engaging life with care and attentiveness in all its complexity rather than attempting to transcend the struggles that we must contend with. Living a good life, according to psychoanalysis, resembles skillfully adapting to the changing conditions we confront rather than arriving at a preordained endpoint. Part of leading a full life entails operating on all cylinders rather than developing narrow parts of ourselves. This self-multidimensionality requires integrating and balancing complementary qualities such as honesty and compassion and rationality and ecstacy, rather than cultivating particular virtues. This also involves living creatively, as I discussed in the first chapter. In addition, one needs to strive to be free even as one must continually confront how one is determined. The good life entails attunement to the other and spirituality as well as cultivation of the self. Living with compassion and empathy, as well as with authenticity and vitality, is crucial to this process.

To the extent that psychoanalysis offers stories about how to live that challenge or enrich the impoverished extant secular or spiritual ones, it will be of continuing interest and importance to people and it will survive. To the extent that it doesn't, people will seek meaning elsewhere—in addictive pursuit of wealth and luxury or surrendering to gurus or fundamentalist groups that foster enslavement and self-alienation as they promise enlightenment and freedom.[37]

"People commonly seek false standards of measurement . . . they seek power, success, and wealth for themselves and admire them in others, and . . . they underestimate what is of true value in life," wrote Freud at the end of his life, as I noted earlier.[38] A posthumanist psychoanalysis that elucidated the life well-lived—creative living, spirituality, ethics, love, and the Good Life—treasures what really matters. And that is what makes life worth living.[39]

NOTES

Epigraph: Stoller, 1985, p. 209.

1. Rubin, 1998, p. 201.

Epigraph: Akhmatova, 1949, p. 68.

1. Freud, 1922, p. 128.

2. Freud, 1915/1916, pp. 146–147.

3. Kunitz, 1995, p. 12.

4. Rubin, 1998. Ulanov (2001), Grotstein (2000), and Eigen's (2001) writings on spirituality and Gabbard's (1996) and Mitchell's (2002) on love, among others, represent a turn, in contemporary psychoanalysis, in a helpful direction.

5. Freud, 1921, p. 138.

6. Rubin, 1998.

7. Ricoeur, 1970.

8. Rosenau (1993) highlights an "affirmative" as opposed to pessimistic postmodernism, which consists of theories and practices that are constructive and visionary as opposed to "eliminative" and "reactive" (p. 16, n.11). There is a tension in postmodernist writings between, on the one hand, an exemplary challenging of authority, a subverting of inequitable hierarchies, and a championing of the subordinated and exiled and, on the other hand, a theorizing that sometimes avoids epistemological accountability and has had and continues to have quietistic implications. Postmodernist claims about the "undecidability" of meaning and the play of "difference(s)" within a text or theory can serve escapist purposes as well as ethical ends. Such notions can be used to sanction cynical disengagement from life or to challenge relations of dominance (Rubin, 1998).

9. McDougall, 1978 & 1994.

10. Freud, 1914a, p. 85.

11. Wilkinson and Gabbard, 1995.

12. Rubin, 1998.

13. Williams, 1989. Discussions with Lou Breger and JoAnn Magdoff enriched the writing of this introduction, as did the editorial comments of Jean Bratman.

NOTES TO CHAPTER ONE

Epigraph: Jung, 1916a/1960, p. 400; para. 789.

1. de Sade, 1966, p. 609; quoted in Bach, 1994, p. 60.

2. Bach, 1994, p. 68.

3. Mannoni, 1972, p. 93.

4. Bach, 1994, p. xv; McDougall, 1980.

5. Freud, 1930, pp. 213–214.

6. Bach, 1994, pp. 3–4.

7. Freud, 1908.

8. Bach, 1994.

9. Freud, 1916–1917, p. 376.

10. Ibid.

11. Freud, 1907. Kris, 1952; Winnicott, 1971; Milner, 1987; McDougall, 1995; and Ogden, 2001 are the exceptions that suggest the rule.

12. Storr, 1988.

13. Freud, 1910.

14. Freud, 1907.

15. Freud, 1907, p. 8.

16. Freud, 1910.

17. Kendrick, 1996, p. 99.

18. Kendrick, 1996, p. 117.

19. Auden, 1939.

20. Jones, 1957, p. 205.

21. Miller, 1987, p. 320.

22. Agee, 1962, p. 127.

23. Mitchell, 1993.

24. Gedo, 1996, p. 97.

25. Rank, 1932.

26. Oremland, 1997, p. 55.

27. Jason Shinder, 2000. The quote from Ntozake Shange is on p. 92. The quote from Susan Wood is on pp. 184–185. The quote from Rebecca Walker is on p. 38.

28. Oremland, 1997, p. 165.

29. Freud, 1926, pp. 154–155.

30. Gehlen, 1980, p. ix.

31. Becker, 1973.

32. Becker, 1973, p. 145.

33. Rothenberg, 1976.

34. Rubin, *The Art of Living,* nd.

35. Jung, 1916a/1960, p. 400; para. 789.

36. Milner, 1967/1987, p. 241.

37. Freud, 1900. Freud did not always fully appreciate the complexity and creativity of the psyche, and, at times, even conceived of it in excessively pathological ways. His claim that dreams are the fulfillment of infantile wishes, for example, reduces their multidimensionality—the manifold functions (creative, prospective, and self-healing)—as well as wish-fulfilling that analysts such as Jung recognized.

38. Rieff, 1959, p. 36.

39. Freud was not the first to make this claim. Myer and Flournoy explored the "mythopoetic function of the unconscious" earlier in the nineteenth century, as Ellenberger (1970, pp. 314 & 317) aptly notes. In her *Darwinism in Morals and Other Essays,* Frances Power Cobbe (1872) says: "We have been accustomed to consider the myth-creating power of the human mind as one especially belonging to the earlier stages of growth of society and of the individual. [But] this instinct exists in every one of us, and exerts itself with more or less energy through the whole of our lives" (p. 132). I am grateful to Rieff (1959) who drew my attention to this passage.

40. Salman, 1997, p. 68. The unconscious, for Fromm (1950) and Loewald (1977), is also a source of creativity and affective density and vibrancy.

41. Jung, 1928/1953.

42. Jung, CW 17, para. 195.

43. There are intimations of the notion of self-healing throughout psychoanalytic history—I am thinking of Ferenczi's "wise baby," the child who becomes a parent to herself and Winnicott's "caretaker self" who protects the vulnerable authentic self from retraumatization. Monte Ullman (1979; 1996; 1999) has explored the creative and self-healing dimension of dreams from an ecumenical, non-Jungian perspective.

44. Jung, CW 6, para. 717.

45. Ibid.

46. Jung, CW 6, para. 701. Jung's thinking was not free of reductionism. In the *Dream Seminars of 1928–30* (e.g., 1984, p. 314), for example, he automatically assumed that the image four in a dream represented the four Jungian functions (thinking, feeling, sensing, and intuition); demonstrating the all-too-human predilection for drawing conclusions that foreclose complexity and creativity.

47. Freud, 1912b, p. 265.

48. Freud, 1900; 1912a.

49. Jung, 1916/1960, p. 67, pp. 82–84, para. 168–171.

50. Bollas, 1992, p. 53. I read Ogden's (2001) evocative discussion of the analyst's "reveries" as his or her "waking dreams" (p. 5) and "waking dream-life" (p. 12) as I was completing the galleys of this manuscript.

51. Oremland, 1997, p. 30.

52. Winnicott, 1971.

53. Khan, 1974, p. 314.

54. Khan, 1974, p. 314.

55. Rubin, 1998.

56. Winnicott, 1971.

57. Winnicott, 1971, p. 26.

58. Winnicott, 1971, p. 35.

59. Winnicott, 1971, p. 33.

60. Khan, 1974, p. 97.

61. Rubin, 1998.

62. I benefited from Dr Marianne Horney Eckardt's reminder about this dimension of creative living (personal communication, December, 2001).

63. Bollas, 1989, p. 212.

64. Oliver, 1992, pp. 10–11.

65. Rubin, 1998, p. 180.

66. In his notion of "radical evaluation," a fundamental questioning of motives, values, and meanings, Jonathan Lear (1990) usefully links the Socrates of *Apology* (38a) and the psychoanalytic project. Discussions with George Atwood, Claude Barbre, Susan Cohen, Doris Dlugacz, Don Kalshed, E. Betty Levin, Louise Reiner, Ann Ulanov, Barry Ulanov, and Victoria Wyndham nourished this chapter. E. Betty Levin freed up my creativity just when it was threatening to remain on holiday for an extended vacation. Extended discussions with Don Kalshed strengthened an earlier draft of this chapter as did Jean Bratman's editorial suggestions. Marianne Horney Eckardt's reading of a penultimate draft opened up new dimensions of the topic. Steven O'Neill, Michelle McKee, and David Ward of the Kristine Mann Library of the Analytical Psychology Club of New York provided able bibliographic assistance—as did Matthew Vonunwerth from the library of the New York Psychoanalytic Institute.

NOTES TO CHAPTER TWO

Epigraph: Taylor, 1989, p. 28.

1. Benjamin, 1990, p. 33.

2. Jung (1933) had actually recognized many years before that psychotherapists had taken on the role of the clergy: "we psychotherapists must occupy ourselves with problems which, strictly speaking, belong to the theologian" (p. 241). Hoffman (1998) has also usefully stressed inevitable moral aspects of the psychoanalytic relationship.

3. Breuer & Freud, 1895, p. 305.

4. Fromm, 1960, p. 86.

5. Jung, Winnicott, Loewald, Grotstein, Ulanov, Eigen, and Marcus, among other analysts, were also interested in something more. They stressed wholeness, creativity, ecstacy, and vitality in living, among other things.

6. Freud, 1933.

7. Fromm, 1947, p. 33.

8. Rubin, 1998.

9. Gedo, 1986, p. 207.

10. Hartmann, 1960.

11. Cushman, 1995, p. 285.

12. Hoffman, 1998, pp. xx–xxi.

13. Because materialism, in the philosophical sense, inhered in Freud's outlook and corpus, the idealist metaphysic I am suggesting may at first blush be unexpected.

14. Kohut, 1977, p. 133 n.15.

15. Rubin, 1998.

16. Rubin, 1998.

17. Benjamin, 1990.

18. Phillips, 1994.

19. Rubin, 1998.

20. Aristotle, 1953, p. 151.

21. Aristotle, 1953, p. 209.

22. Bernstein, 1986, p. 99.

23. Gadamer, 1976, p. 201.

24. Bernstein, 1986, p. 55.

25. Aristotle, 1953, pp. 211–212 ft. 3.

26. Bernstein, 1986, p. 101.

27. Gadamer, 1975, pp. 34 & 36.

28. Levi-Strauss, 1966.

29. Levi-Strauss, 1966, p. 17.

30. Kohut, 1978, p. 609.

31. I am using Levi-Strauss (1966) strategically, valuing his metaphor of bricolage, without subscribing to his unconvincing binary opposition between the primitive bricoleur and the sophisticated engineer.

32. Freud, 1930, p. 64.

33. Finn & Gartner, 1992; Sorenson, 1994; Jones, 1996; Spezzano & Gargiulo, 1997; Marcus, 2003.

34. Suler, 1993; Rubin, 1996; 1998; Molino, 1998. Magid, 2002; Safran, 2003; Segal, 2003.

35. Ricoeur, 1970.

36. Rubin, 1996.

37. Rubin, 1997.

38. Freud, 1917.

39. Foucault, 1980.

40. There are echoes here of Foucault's (1983) focus on the aesthetics of the self.

41. Berlin, 1953, p. 1.

42. Gadamer, 1976.

43. Bernstein, 1992, p. 339.

44. Strenger, 1997, p. 69.

45. Alford, 1990, p. 154.

46. Bernstein, 1992, p. 328.

47. Blake, 1993, "Proverbs of Hell," p. 39.

48. Prilletensky, 1997.

49. Jones, 1998, p. 3.

50. Fromm, 1947, p. 30.

51. Fromm, 1947, p. 119.

52. Aristotle and Spinoza conceived of self-love as a virtue (e.g., Fromm, 1947, p. 123).

53. Benjamin, 1995, p. 30.

54. 1945, p. 62. This is an enlarged and expanded version of two earlier essays (Rubin 1997a; 2001). Discussions with Peter Carnochan, James Jones, Joel Kramer, Doris Dlugacz, Louis Breger, and JoAnn Magdoff were very helpful in the development of this chapter.

NOTES TO CHAPTER THREE

Epigraph: Freud, 1914a; Sexton, 1981.

1. Mitchell, 1997.

2. Taylor, 1991.

3. Todorov, 1997, p. 381.

4. Erikson, 1950, p. 264.

5. Gaylin & Person, 1988, p. ix.

6. Altman, 1977; Balint, 1948; Bergmann, 1980.

7. Gabbard, 1996, p. 16. Suttie (1935), Lear (1990), Gabbard (1996), and Mitchell (2002) are four exceptions suggesting the generalization. Suttie recognized the omission of love in classical analytic theory, especially the taboo of tenderness (p. 4). He placed love, rather than aim-inhibited sexuality, as primary. Speaking of contemporary analysis, and attempting to flesh out implications that he feels are latent, but not fully elaborated in Freud, Lear (1990) notes: "[L]ove has become almost taboo within psychoanalysis" (p.15), despite the fact that it is a "basic natural force" in the universe (p. 210), one that

"promotes the development of ever more complex unities" (p. 212) and is the enabling condition for a person to come into being.

8. Wordsworth, 1984.

9. The use of the word couples refers to same-sex as well as heterosexual unions.

10. Rubin, 1998.

11. There are, of course, sociocultural as well as intrapsychic and interpersonal obstacles to intimacy. Cognitive oversaturation and two-family employment literally sap couples of physical and emotional energy for closeness.

12. Schafer, 1976.

13. Ricoeur, 1970.

14. Klein (1975) and Gabbard (1996) are exceptions. "Hate is often used as the most effective cover for love" (p. 260), as Klein notes.

15. Freud, 1921, p. 138.

16. Mitchell, 1997, p. 24.

17. Benjamin, 1995, p. 29.

18. Rubin, 1996; 1998.

19. Yalom, 1989.

20. Gaylin & Person, 1988, pp. 5–6.

21. Freud, 1915, p. 168.

22. Ibid.

23. Freud, 1912.

24. Kernberg, 1995.

25. Ibid.

26. Fairbairn, 1943, pp. 66–67.

27. Bach, 1994.

28. Benjamin, 1988.

29. Bach, 1994, p. 46.

30. Mitchell, 1997; 2002.

31. McKeon, 1954, p. 32.

32. King James Bible, St. Paul, I. Corinthians, p. 155.

33. Pascal, 1958, p. 110; par. 416.

34. Pascal, 1958, p. 107; par. 398.

35. Auden, 1939, p. 533.

36. Wilkinson & Gabbard, 1995.

37. Wilkinson & Gabbard, 1995, p. 210.

38. The writings of Winnicott, 1971; Ogden, 1986; Phillips, 1988; Bollas, 1992; and Bach, 1994 contributed to my conception of potential space.

39. Todorov, 1996.

40. Ogden, 1986.

41. Bach, 1994, p. xvii.

42. Bach, 1994, p. 56.

43. Zuckerberg, 1985.

44. Plato in *Gorgias* 507c and Aristotle, *Nicomachean Ethics* 1144b32ff.

45. Modell, 1990.

46. Benjamin, 1995.

47. Forster, 1921, pp. 194–195.

48. Winnicott, 1986.

49. W. B Yeats, 1971, p. 513.

50. Ulanov & Ulanov, 1994, p. 89.

51. Borges, 1952, p. 99.

52. Fromm, 1956, pp. 4–5.

53. Barthes, 1978.

54. Auden took this out of the published version, perhaps acknowledging that we die anyhow. Nonetheless, he was pointing, like the late Freud, to the importance, and healing properties, of love. The feedback of Diana Alstad, Robin Cohen, Susan Cohen, Doris Dlugacz, Joel Kramer, David Kastan, Dorthy Levinson, Mary Traina, and Barry Ulanov enriched this chapter. I am also grateful to Jim Barron and the two anonymous readers from *Gender and Psychoanalysis* whose suggestions improved a penultimate draft.

NOTES TO CHAPTER FOUR

1. Ulanov, 1985; Symington, 1994; Roland, 1996; Rubin, 1996; 1998; Spezzano & Garguilo, 1997; Eigen, 1998; Grotstein, 2000; Marcus, 2003.

2. Freud, 1927.

3. Barbre, 1998, p. 176.

4. Alexander, 1931.

5. Jung, 1933.

6. Freud, 1927.

7. Milner, 1973.

8. Levin, 1987, p. 3.

9. Kovel, 1990, p. 80.

10. I am grateful to Randy Sorenson's comments on desecularization and modernity in a lecture on psychoanalysis and religion at the August 2000 meeting of Division 36 of the American Psychological Association in Washington, DC.

11. Symington, 1994.

12. L. L. Whyte quoted in Highwater, 1981, p. xii.

13. Quoted in Moncayo, 1998, p. 4.

14. Wittgenstein, 1953.

15. Freud, 1930, p. 64.

16. Rubin, 1998.

17. Freud, 1927, p. 27.

18. Stolorow & Atwood, 1979; Rubin, 1998; Breger, 2000.

19. Rubin, 1999.

20. Bettelheim, 1982.

21. Schafer, 1976.

22. Freud, 1927.

23. Corbett, 1996, p. 168.

24. Rubin, 1996; 1998.

25. I read Grotstein's (2000) writings on a fourth position, a "transcendent position," characterized by serenity and reconciliation with the universe, as I was preparing to submit this manuscript. Spirituality is, for Grotstein (2000), the "latent capacity within imperfect subjects for attaining full development" (p. xxvi). He terms the "state of serenity" in which one becomes "reconciled to the experience of pure, unadultered Being and Happening"—with an obvious nod to Melanie Klein and the post-Kleinian revisions of Thomas Ogden—the "transcendent position" (p. 282).

26. Rubin, 1998.

27. I am indebted to Neil Altman, who first inspired this way of thinking about psychoanalysis.

28. Freud, 1900, 1912a; Horney, 1987; Kelman, 1960; Bion, 1970; and Rubin, 1985, 1996.

29. Freud, 1900; 1912a.

30. Rubin, 1985; 1996.

31. Horney, 1987.

32. Horney, 1987, p. 35.

33. Horney, 1987. p. 18.

34. Kelman, 1960.

35. Bion, 1970, pp. 51–52.

36. Although Bion did not speak explicitly about spirituality, his thinking and theorizing are comparable with it. Bion's "O" refers to ultimate, unknowable reality, including the ineffable mystical. His theorizing is an attempt to depict and not reduce actuality.

37. Suzuki, 1970, p. 21.

38. Mitchell & Black, 1995, p. 195.

39. Ferenczi, 1927, p. 79.

40. Ghent, 1990, p. 125.

41. Ghent, 1990, p. 111.

42. Jung, 1938, p. 7, par. 6.

43. Jung, 1938, p. 8, par. 9.

44. Winnicott, [1951]1978.

45. Winnicott, [1951]1978, p. 230

46. Winnicott, [1951]1978, p. 231.

47. Winnicott, [1951]1978, p. 230.

48. Rubin, 1998.

49. Ulanov, 1985.

50. Epstein, 1995.

51. Boucher, 1988.

52. Rubin, 1996; 1998.

53. Buddhaghosa, 1976.

54. Narada, 1975.

55. Ibid.

56. Rubin, 1996, p. 130.

57. Narada, 1975; Buddhaghosa, 1976.

58. Goldstein, 1976; Goleman, 1977; Kornfield, 1977; Walsh, 1981.

59. Rubin, 1996.

60. Roland, 1996, p. xvi.

61. Roland, 1996.

62. Rubin, 1996; 1998; 1999.

63. Suzuki, 1970.

64. Kenyon, 1996, pp. 190–191.

65. Kramer & Alstad, 1993.

66. Nietzsche, [1887] 1967.

67. Wittgenstein, 1980, p. 50e.

68. Ozick, 1983, p. 203.

69. Ozick, 1983, p. 202.

70. Kierkegaard, 1843/1941, p. 52.

71. Rubin, 1998.

72. Eigen's (2001) poetic depiction of spirituality and mysticism aided me in articulating my own sense of spiritual experiences, particularly their bliss and radiance.

73. Winnicott's ([1951] 1978) reflections on transitional objects and transitional
phenomena played a seminal role in my conception of spiritual experience. Creativity,
not spirituality, was emphasized by Winnicott in his reflections on transitional experiencing. My work could be viewed, at least in part, as a spiritualizing of Winnicott's.

74. Symington, 1994.

75. Freud, 1927, p. 53.

76. Jones, 1996.

77. Bollas 1997, pp. 48–49.

78. Langs & Searles, 1980.

79. Burke, 1950.

80. Rubin, 1996; 1998.

81. Smith, 1982, p. 178. This chapter was inspired by Mark Finn and benefited from
discussions with Diana Alstad, Neil Altman, Emma Anderson, Jim Barron, Claude
Barbre, Mark Branitsky, Lou Breger, Peter Carnochan, Paul Cooper, Doris Dlugacz,

Mark Finn, Jerry Garguilo, Jim Jones, Don Kalshed, Joel Kramer, Barry Magid, Esther Menaker, Louise Reiner, Alan Roland, Tony Schwartz, Mary Traina, Ann and Barry Ulanov, and Avi Winokur. I am especially grateful to Neil Altman and Barry Magid, whose feedback on a penultimate draft greatly enriched this chapter.

NOTES TO CHAPTER FIVE

Epigraph: Schuyler, 1993, p. 214.

1. Fromm, 1995, p. 17.

2. Rubin, 1996.

3. Rubin, 1996.

4. Schafer, 1976.

5. Schafer, 1976, p. 47.

6. Schafer, 1976.

7. Winnicott, 1971, p. 98.

8. W. H. Auden, 1963, p. 6.

9. Rubin, 1998.

10. Ricoeur, 1970.

11. Fromm, 1998.

12. Farber, 1976.

13. Novick, 1997.

14. Orwell, 1949/1981, p. 176.

15. Ibid.

16. Koren, 1994, p. 7.

17. Dickinson, 1957, p. 8.

18. cummings, 1972, p. 775.

19. Klein, 1960/1975.

20. Thomas Ogden's (1994) suggestive reading of Melanie Klein was instrumental in the formulation of my own view of the implications in her work for mental health.

21. Ferenczi, 1928/1980, pp. 98–99.

22. Ferenczi, 1927/1980, p. 79.

23. Murphy, 1992.

24. Rorty, 1986, p. 11.

25. Ibid.

26. Rorty, 1986, p. 12.

27. Phillips, 1998, p. xvi.

28. Mitchell's (2000) reading of Loewald sharpened my sense of his alternative conception of health. Loewald regarded conventional ideals and norms of health involving living adaptively with maturity, rationality, and self-control as a stale and shallow

existence, bleached of depth and vitality. Health, for Loewald, entailed a life in which self and other, fantasy and reality, past and present are linked as well as differentiated so that they might mutually influence and enrich each other.

29. Mitchell, 1993; Rubin, 1996; Hoffman, 1998; Bromberg, 1998; Rubin, 1998; and Eigen, 2001. A diverse group of psychoanalytic feminists—Adrienne Harris, Virginia Goldner, Jody Davies, Muriel Dimen, and Jessica Benjamin—have made an important contribution to discussions of multiplicity in regard to gender.

30. Gay, 1990, p. 89.

31. Loewald, 1978.

32. Wallwork, 1988, p. 203.

33. Mitchell, 1997, p. 320; Bromberg, 1998. I hope it is clear that in my view there does not have to be a split or cleavage between interpersonal and object relations theorists. They are often describing interpenetrating aspects of experience that are linked in a dialogue of mutual influence.

34. Rubin, 1996; 1998.

35. From my Loewaldian (1960; 1974) perspective, in which past and present, fantasy and reality, primary process and secondary process interweave, the present can be reanimated and enriched (as well as haunted by) the past. Fromm's (1956) claim that any vestiges of oedipal childhood passion hinder adult love could be devitalizing and sterile.

36. Kohut, 1985. Erikson (1968) described life as a struggle toward greater wisdom and virtue.

37. Rubin, 1998.

38. Freud, 1930, p. 64. This chapter was enriched by dialogues with Jerry Gold, Jo Ann Magdoff, and Louise Reiner.

BIBLIOGRAPHY

Ackerman, S., & Macklin, J. (1998). *The Book of Love*. New York: W. W. Norton.

Agee, J. (1962). *Letters of James Agee to Father Flye*. New York: George Braziller.

Akhmatova, A. (1949). *Poems*. Trans. Lyn Coffin. New York: W. W. Norton, 1983.

Alexander, F. (1931). Buddhistic training as an artificial catatonia. *Psychoanalytic Review*, 18: 129–145.

Alford, C. F. (1990). Psychoanalysis, relativism, and morality. *American Imago*, 47(2): 145–167.

Altman, L. (1977). Some vicissitudes of love. *Journal of the American Psychoanalytic Association*, 25: 35–42.

Aristotle. (322 B.C.E.). *Nicomachean Ethics*. Trans. J. A. K. Thomson. New York: Penguin Books, 1953.

Auden, W. H. (1939). In Memory of W. B. Yeats. In G. Roelofs (Ed.), *The Major Poets: English and American*. New York: Harcourt, Brace & World.

———. (1939). In Memory of Sigmund Freud. In *Collected Shorter Poems 1927–1957*. New York: Vintage Books, 1975, pp. 166–170.

———. (1963). *The Dyer's Hand*. London: Faber.

———. (1969). *Epistles to a Godson and Other Poems*. New York: Random House.

Bach, S. (1994). *The Language of Perversion and the Language of Love*. Northvale, NJ: Jason Aronson.

Balint, M. (1948). On genital love. *International Journal of Psycho-Analysis*, 28: 34–40.

Barbre, C. (1998). Review of psychotherapy and the sacred: Religious experience and religious resources in psychotherapy. *Journal of Religion and Health*, 37(2): 176–177.

Barthes, R. (1978). *A Lover's Discourse: Fragments*. New York: Hill and Wang.

Bass, A. (1998). Sigmund Freud: The Question of a Weltanschauung. In P. Marcus. & A. Rosenberg (Eds), *Psychoanalytic Versions of the Human Condition*. New York: New York University Press, pp. 412–446.

Becker, E. (1973). *Denial of Death*. New York: Free Press.

Bender, S. (1995). *Everyday Sacred: A Women's Journey Home*. San Francisco: Harper-Collins.

Benjamin, J. (1988). *The Bonds of Love: Psychoanalysis, Feminism, and the Problem of Domination.* New York: Pantheon Books.

———. (1990). An outline of intersubjectivity: The development of mutual recognition. *Psychoanalytic Psychology,* 7 (Suppl.): 33–46

———. (1995). *Like Subjects, Love Objects.* New Haven & London: Yale University Press.

Bergmann, M. (1980). On the intrapsychic function of falling in love. *Psychoanalytic Quarterly,* 44: 56–77.

Berlin, I. (1951). *Russian Thinkers.* Harmondsworth, England: Penguin, 1978.

Bernstein, R. (1986). *Philosophical Profiles.* Philadelphia: University of Pennsylvania Press.

———. (1992). *The New Constellation: The Ethical-Political Horizons of Modernity/Postmodernity.* Cambridge: MIT Press.

Bettelheim, B. (1982). *Freud and Man's Soul.* New York: Random House.

Bion, W. (1970). *Attention and Interpretation.* New York: Basic Books.

Blake, W. (1993). Proverbs of Hell. In *Selected Poems.* Rutland, Vermont: Charles Tuttle.

Bollas, C. (1989). *Forces of Destiny: Psychoanalysis and Human Idiom.* London: Free Association Books.

———. (1992). *Being a Character: Psychoanalysis and Self Experience.* New York: Hill & Wang.

———. (1995). *Cracking Up: The Work of Unconscious Experience.* New York: Hill and Wang.

———. (1996). Figures and their functions: On the oedipal structure of a psychoanalysis. *Psychoanalytic Quarterly,* 65(1): 1–20.

———. (1997). Interview with Anthony Molino. In *Freely Associated: Encounters in Psychoanalysis with Christopher Bollas, Joyce McDougall, Michael Eigen, Adam Phillips, and Nina Coltart.* London: Free Association Books, pp. 5–51.

Borges, J-L. (1952). The Meeting in a Dream. In *Other Inquisitions* (1937–1952). Austin: University of Texas Press, pp. 97–100.

Boucher, S. (1988). *Turning the Wheel: American Women Creating the New Buddhism.* San Francisco: Harper and Row.

Bratzlav, N. (1996). The Torah of the Void. In C. Milosz (Ed.), *A Book of Luminous Things.* New York: Harcourt, Brace & Company.

Breger, L. (2000). *Freud: Darkness in the Midst of Vision—An Analytical Biography.* New York: John Wiley.

Breuer, J., & Freud, S. (1895). Studies on Hysteria. *S.E.:* 2. London: Hogarth Press.

Bromberg, P. (1998). *Standing in the Spaces: Essays on Clinical Process, Trauma, and Dissociation.* Hillsdale, NJ: Analytic Press.

Browning, R. (1954). "Love Among the Ruins." In G. Roelofs (Ed.), *The Major Poets: English and American.* New York: Harcourt, Brace & World, pp. 361–363.

Buddhaghosa, B. (1976). *The Path of Purification.* Trans. B. Nyanamoli. Berkeley: Shambhala.

Burke, K. (1969). *A Rhetoric of Motives.* Berkeley: University of California Press.

Corbett, L. (1996). *The Religious Function of the Psyche.* New York: Routledge.

cummings, e. e. (1972). *Complete Poems*. New York: Harcourt, Brace Jovanovich.

Cushman, P. (1995). *Constructing the Self, Constructing America*. New York: Addison-Wesley.

Davies, J. M. (1996). Linking the "pre-analytic" with the post-classical: Integration, dissociation, and the multiplicity of unconscious process. *Contemporary Psychoanalysis*, 32: 553–576.

Derrida, J. (1981). *Positions*. Chicago: University of Chicago Press.

Dickinson, E. (1957). *Poems*. Boston: Little, Brown.

Dimen, M. (1991). Deconstructing difference: Gender, splitting and transitional space. *Psychoanalytic Dialogues*, 1: 335–352.

Dunn, S. (1998). Poets, poetry, and the spiritual. *Georgia Review*, 52(2): 269–284.

Eigen, M. (1998). *The Psychoanalytic Mystic*. Binghamton, NY: ESF Publishers.

———. (2001). *Ecstasy*. Middleton, CT: Wesleyan University Press.

Eliot, T. S. (1963). Four Quartets. In *Collected Poems (1909–1962)*. New York: Harcourt, Brace & World.

Elliott, A., & Spezzano, C. (1996). Psychoanalysis at its limits: Navigating the postmodern turn. *Psychoanalytic Quarterly*, 65(1): 52–83.

Ellenberger, H. (1970). *The Discovery of the Unconscious: The History and Evolution of Dynamic Psychiatry*. New York: Basic Books.

Epstein, M. (1995). *Thoughts without a Thinker: Psychotherapy from a Buddhist Perspective*. New York: Basic Books.

Erikson, E. (1950). *Childhood and Society*. New York: W. W. Norton.

———. (1968). *Identity: Youth and Crisis*. New York: W. W. Norton.

Fairbairn, R. (1943). The Repression and the Return of Bad Objects (with special reference to the 'War Neuroses'). In *Psychoanalytic Studies of the Personality*. London: Routledge & Kegan Paul, pp. 59–81.

Farber, L. (1976). *Lying, Despair, Jealousy, Envy, Sex, Suicide, Drugs, and the Good Life*. New York: Basic Books.

Ferenczi, S. (1927/1980). The Problem of the Termination of the Analysis. In *Final Contributions to the Problems and Methods of Psycho-Analysis*. New York: Brunner/Mazel, pp. 77–86.

———. (1928/1980). The Elasticity of Psychoanalytic Technique. In *Final Contributions to the Problems and Methods of Psycho-Analysis*. New York: Brunner/Mazel, pp. 87–101.

Finn, M., & Gartner, J. (Eds.)(1992). *Object Relations Theory and Religious Experience*. Westport, CT: Praeger.

Forster, E. M. (1921). *Howard's End*. New York: Vintage Books.

Foucault, M. (1980). Two Lectures. In Colin Gordan (Ed.), *Power/Knowledge: Selected Interviews and Other Writings* (1972–1977). New York: Pantheon, pp. 78–108.

———. (1983). *The Care of the Self*. Trans. Robert Hurley. New York: Random House.

Freud, S. (1900). The Interpretation of Dreams. *S. E.*: 4–5. London: Hogarth Press.

———. (1907). Delusion and Dreams in Jensen's Gradiva. *S. E.*: 9: 3–95. London: Hogarth Press.

———. (1908). Creative Writers and Day-Dreaming. *S. E.*: 9:143–153. London: Hogarth Press.

———. (1910). Leonardo da Vinci and a Memory of His Childhood. *S. E.*: 11: 57–137. London: Hogarth Press.

———. (1912). On the Universal Tendency to Debasement in the Sphere of Love. *S. E.*: 11: 177–190. London: Hogarth Press.

———. (1912a). Recommendations to Physicians Practicing Psycho-Analysis. *S. E.*: 12: 111–120. London: Hogarth Press.

———. (1912b). A Note on the Unconscious in Psycho-Analysis. *S. E.*: 12: 260–266. London: Hogarth Press.

———. (1914). The *Moses* of Michelangelo. *S. E.*: 13: 211–238. London: Hogarth Press.

———. (1914a). On Narcissism: An Introduction. *S. E.*: 14: 67–102. London: Hogarth Press.

———. (1915). Observations on Transference-Love. *S. E.*: 12: 157–173. London: Hogarth Press.

———. (1915/1916). Introductory Lectures on Psycho-Analysis. *S. E.*: 15. London: Hogarth Press.

———. (1916–1917). Introductory Lectures on Psycho-Analysis. *S. E.*: 16: 243–476. London: Hogarth Press.

———. (1917). A Difficulty in the Path of Psychoanalysis. *S. E.*: 17: 135–144. London: Hogarth Press.

———. (1921). Group Psychology and the Analysis of the Ego. *S. E.*: 18: 67–143. London: Hogarth Press.

———. (1922). Two Encyclopedic Articles: Psychoanalysis. *S. E.*: 18: 235–259. London: Hogarth Press.

———. (1925). Negation. *S. E.*: 19: 235–239. London: Hogarth Press.

———. (1926). Inhibitions, Symptoms and Anxiety. *S. E.*: 20: 87–175. London: Hogarth Press.

———. (1927). The Question of Lay Analysis. *S. E.*: 20: 183–258. London: Hogarth Press.

———. (1927). The Future of an Illusion. *S. E.*: 21. London: Hogarth Press.

———. (1928). Dostoevsky and Parricide. *S. E.*: 21: 175–196. London: Hogarth Press.

———. (1930). Appendix: List of Writings by Freud Dealing Mainly or Largely with Art, Literature or the Theory of Aesthetics. *S. E.*: 21: 213–214. London: Hogarth Press.

———. (1930). Civilization and Its Discontents. S.E.: 21: 64–145. London: Hogarth Press.

———. (1933). New Introductory Lectures on Psycho-Analysis. S.E.: 22: 5–182. London: Hogarth Press.

———. (1937). Analysis Terminable and Interminable. *S. E.*: 23: 209–253. London: Hogarth Press.

————. (1954). *The Origins of Psycho-Analysis: Letters to Wilhelm Fliess, Drafts, and Notes.* Marie Bonaparte, Anna Freud, & Ernest Kris (Eds.), Trans. Eric Mosbacher & James Strachey. New York: Basic Books.

————. (1960). *The Letters of Sigmund Freud.* E. Freud (Ed.), Trans. Tania Stern & James Stern. New York: Basic Books.

————. (1963). *Psychoanalysis and Faith: Dialogues with the Reverend Oskar Pfister.* H. Meng & E. Freud (Eds.). New York: Basic Books.

Frisch, M. (1982). *Gantenbein.* New York: Harcourt, Brace.

Fromm, E. (1947). *Man for Himself: An Inquiry into the Psychology of Ethics.* New York: Holt, Rinehart & Winston.

————. (1950). *Psychoanalysis and Religion.* New York: Bantam Books, 1972.

————. (1956). *The Art of Loving.* New York: Harper & Row.

————. (1986). *For the Love of Life.* New York: Free Press.

————. (1995). *The Essential Erich Fromm.* New York: Continuum.

————. (1998). *The Art of Being.* New York: Continuum.

————, Suzuki, D.T., & DeMartino, R. (Eds.) (1960). *Zen Buddhism and Psychoanalysis.* New York: Harper and Row.

Gabbard, G. (1996). *Love and Hate in the Analytic Setting.* Northvale, NJ: Jason Aronson.

Gadamer, H.-G. (1975). The Problem of Historical Consciousness. Trans. J. Close. *Graduate Faculty Philosophy Journal,* 5(1): 8–52.

————. (1976). *Philosophical Hermeneutics.* Berkeley: University of California Press.

Gay, P. (1990). Freud and Freedom. In *Reading Freud: Explorations and Entertainments.* New Haven & London: Yale University Press, pp. 74–94.

Gaylin, W., & Person, E. (Eds.)(1988). *Passionate Attachments: Thinking about Love.* New York: Free Press.

Gedo, J. (1986). *Conceptual Issues in Psychoanalysis.* Hillsdale, NJ: Analytic Press.

————. (1989). *Portraits of the Artist.* Hillsdale, NJ: Analytic Press.

————. (1996). *The Artist and the Emotional World.* New York: Columbia University Press.

Gehlen, A. (1980). *Man in the Age of Technology.* Trans. Patricia Lipscomb. New York: Columbia University Press.

Ghent, E. (1990). Masochism, Submission, Surrender. *Contemporary Psychoanalysis,* 26(1): 108–136.

Gilligan, C., & Stern, E. (1988). The Riddle of Femininity and the Psychology of Love. In W. Gaylin & E. Person (Eds.), *Passionate Attachments: Thinking about Love.* New York: Free Press, pp. 101–114.

Goldner, V. (1991). Toward a critical relational theory of gender. *Psychoanalytic Dialogues,* 1: 249–272.

Goldstein, J. (1976). *The Experience of Insight: A Natural Unfolding.* Santa Cruz, CA: Unity Press.

Goleman, D. (1977). *The Varieties of the Meditative Experience.* New York: Dutton.

Grotstein, J. (2000). *Who Is the Dreamer Who Dreams the Dream?: A Study of Psychic Presences*. Hillsdale, NJ: Analytic Press.

Habermas, J. (1971). *Knowledge and Human Interests*. Boston: Beacon Press.

Harris, A. (1991). Gender as contradiction. *Psychoanalytic Dialogues*, 1: 197–224.

Hartmann, H. (1960). *Psychoanalysis and Moral Values*. New York: International Universities Press.

Highwater, J. (1981). *The Primal Mind: Vision and Reality in Indian America*. New York: New American Library.

Hoffman, I. (1998). *Ritual and Spontaneity in the Psychoanalytic Process*. Hillsdale, NJ: Analytic Press.

James, W. (1928). *Varieties of Religious Experience*. New York: Longmans, Green.

Jones, E. (1957). *The Life and Work of Sigmund Freud*. Vol. 3. New York: Basic Books.

Jones, J. (1996). *Religion and Psychology in Transition: Psychoanalysis, Feminism, and Theology*. New Haven: Yale University Press.

———. (1998). The Moral Implications of Psychoanalysis: Discussion of papers by Jeffrey B. Rubin, Peter Carnochan, and Peter Shabad. American Psychological Association Division 39 Meeting, August 1998, San Francisco.

Jung, C. G. (1916/1960). The Transcendent Function. In *The Structure and Dynamics of the Psyche*. Collected Works: 8. Princeton: Princeton University Press, pp. 67–91.

———. (1916a/1960). The Stages of Life. In *The Structure and Dynamics of the Psyche*. Collected Works: 8. Princeton: Princeton University Press, pp. 387–403.

———. (1928/1953). The Synthetic or Constructive Method. In *Two Essays on Analytical Psychology*. Collected Works: 7. Princeton: Princeton University Press, pp. 79–87.

———. (1933). Psychotherapists or Clergy? In *Modern Man in Search of a Soul*. New York: Harcourt, Brace and World, pp. 221–244.

———. (1938). Psychology and Religion. In *Psychology and Religion: West and East*. Collected Works, 11: 3–107. New York: Pantheon.

———. (1973). *C. G. Jung: Letters* I: 1906–1950. Princeton: Princeton University Press.

———. (1984). *Dream Analysis: Notes of the Seminar Given in 1928–1930*. W. McGuire (Ed.). Princeton: Princeton University Press.

Kelman, H. (1960). Psychoanalytic Thought and Eastern Wisdom. In J. Ehrenwald (Ed.), *The History of Psychotherapy*. New York: Jason Aronson.

Kendrick, W. (1996). Writing the Unconscious. In Laurie Adams & Jacques Szaluta (Eds.), *Psychoanalysis and the Humanities*. New York: Brunner/Mazel, pp. 97–118.

Kenyon, J. (1996). Having it Out With Melancholy. In *Otherwise: New and Selected Poems*. Saint Paul, MN: Graywolf Press.

Kernberg, O. (1988). Between Conventionality and Aggression. In W. Gaylin & E. Person (Eds.), *Passionate Attachments: Thinking about Love*. New York: Free Press, pp. 63–83.

———. (1995). *Love Relations: Normality and Pathology*. New Haven: Yale University Press.

Khan, M. (1974). Towards an Epistemology of Cure. In *The Privacy of the Self: Papers on Psychoanalytic Theory and Technique*. New York: International Universities Press, pp. 93–98.

————. (1974b).The Use and Abuse of Dream in Psychic Experience. In *The Privacy of the Self: Papers on Psychoanalytic Theory and Technique*. New York: International Universities Press, pp. 306–315.

Kierkegaard, S. (1843/1941). *Fear and Trembling*. Princeton: Princeton University Press.

Klein, M. (1960/1975). On Mental Health. In *Envy and Gratitude and Other Works (1946–1963)*. New York: Dell.

————. (1975). On Criminality. In *Love, Guilt, and Reparation and Other Works* (1921–1945). New York: Delacorte/Seymour Lawrence Press.

Kohut, H. (1977). *The Restoration of the Self*. New York: International Universities Press.

————. (1978). *The Search for the Self*. New York: International Universities Press.

————. (1985) *Self Psychology and the Humanities*. Charles Strozier (Ed.). New York: W.W. Norton.

Koren, L. (1994). *Wabi-Sabi for Artists, Designers, Poets and Philosophers*. Berkeley, CA: Stone Bridge Press.

Kornfield, J. (1977). *Living Buddhist Masters*. Santa Cruz, CA: Unity Press.

Kovel, J. (1990). Beyond the future of an illusion: Further reflections on Freud and religion. *Psychoanalytic Review*, 77 (1): 69–87.

Kramer, J., & Alstad, D. (1993). *The Guru Papers: Masks of Authoritarian Power*. Berkeley, CA: North Atlantic Press.

Kris, E. (1952). *Psychoanalytic Explorations in Art*. New York: International Universities Press.

Kristeva, J. (1982). *Powers of Horror: An Essay on Abjection*. New York: Columbia University Press.

Kunitz, S. (1995). *Passing Through: The Later Poems*. New York: W.W. Norton.

Langs, R., & Searles, H. (1980). *Intrapsychic and Interpersonal Dimensions of Treatment*. New York: Jason Aronson.

Lear, J. (1990). *Love and Its Place in Nature: A Philosophical Interpretation of Freudian Analysis*. New York: Farrar, Straus & Giroux.

Levin, D. M. (Ed.) (1987). *Pathologies of the Modern Self: Postmodern Studies on Narcissism, Schizophrenia, and Depression*. New York: New York University Press.

Levi-Strauss, C. (1966). *The Savage Mind*. Chicago: University of Chicago Press.

Loewald, H. (1960). On the Therapeutic Action of Psychoanalysis. In *Papers on Psychoanalysis*. New Haven: Yale University Press, 1980, pp. 221–256.

————. (1974). Psychoanalysis as an Art and the Fantasy Character of the Analytic Situation. In *Papers on Psychoanalysis*. New Haven: Yale University Press, 1980, pp. 352–371.

————. (1977). Primary Process, Secondary Process and Language. In *Papers on Psychoanalysis*. New Haven: Yale University Press, 1980, pp. 178–206.

————. (1978). *Psychoanalysis and the History of the Individual*. New Haven & London: Yale University Press.

Magid, B. (2002). *Ordinary Mind: Exploring the Common Ground of Zen and Psychoanalysis*. Boston: Wisdom Publications.

Mannoni. O. (1972). Psychoanalysis and the Decolonization of Mankind. In Jonathan Miller (Ed), *Freud: The Man, His World, His Influence*. Boston: Little, Brown, pp. 85–95.

Marcus, P. (2003). *Ancient Religious Wisdom, Spirituality, and Psychoanalysis*. Westport, CT: Praeger.

McDougall, J. (1980). *A Plea for a Measure of Abnormality*. New York: International Universities Press.

———. (1995). *The Many Faces of Eros: A Psychoanalytic Exploration of Human Sexuality*. New York.: W. W. Norton.

McKeon, R. (1954). Love and Philosophical Analysis. In *Thought, Action, and Passion*. Chicago: University of Chicago Press, pp. 30–53.

Meltzer, F. (1987). Editor's introduction: Partitive plays, pipe dreams. *Critical Inquiry*, 13(2): 215–221.

Miller, A. (1987). *Time Bends: A Life*. New York: Grove Press.

Milner, M. ([1973]1987). Some Notes on Psychoanalytic Ideas about Mysticism. In *The Suppressed Madness of Sane Men: Forty Four Years of Exploring Psychoanalysis*. London: Tavistock Publications, pp. 258–274.

———. ([1975]1987). A Discussion of Masud Khan's paper 'In Search of the Dreaming Experience.' In *The Suppressed Madness of Sane Men*. London: Tavistock Publications, pp. 275–278.

———. (1987). *The Suppressed Madness of Sane Men*. London: Tavistock Publications.

Mitchell, S. (1993). *Hope and Dread in Psychoanalysis*. New York: Basic Books.

———. (1997). *Influence and Autonomy in Psychoanalysis*. Hillsdale, NJ: Analytic Press.

———. (1997). Psychoanalysis and the Degradation of Romance. *Psychoanalytic Dialogues*, 7(1): 23–41.

———. (2000). *Relationality: From Attachment to Intersubjectivity*. Hillsdale, NJ: Analytic Press.

———. (2002). *Can Love Last? The Fate of Romance over Time*. New York & London: W. W. Norton.

———, & Black, M. (1995). *Freud and Beyond: A History of Modern Psychoanalytic Thought*. New York: Basic Books.

Modell, A. (1990). *Other Minds, Other Realities: Toward a Theory of Psychoanalytic Treatment*. Cambridge: Harvard University Press.

Molino, T. (Ed.) (1998). *The Couch and the Tree: Dialogues in Psychoanalysis and Buddhism*. New York: North Point Press.

Moncayo, R. (1998). Psychoanalysis and postmodern spirituality. *Journal for the Psychoanalysis of Culture and Society*, 3(2): 1–7.

Murphy, M. (1992). *The Future of the Body*. Los Angeles: Tarcher.

Narada, T. (1975). *A Manual of Abhidhamma*. Columbo, Sri Lanka: Buddhist Publication Society.

Nehemas, A. (1998). *The Art of Living: Socratic Reflections from Plato to Foucault*. Princeton: Princeton University Press.

Nietzsche, F. ([1887]1967). *On the Genealogy of Morals.* Trans. W. Kaufmann. New York: Random House.

Novick, J. (1997). Termination conceivable and inconceivable. *Psychoanalytic Psychology,* 14: 145–162.

Nozick, R. (1989). *The Examined Life: Philosophical Meditations.* New York: Simon & Schuster.

Ogden, T. (1986). *The Matrix of Mind: Object Relations and the Psychoanalytic Dialogue.* Northvale, NJ: Jason Aronson.

———. (1994). *Subjects of Analysis.* Northvale, NJ/London: Jason Aronson.

———. (2001). *Conversations at the Frontier of Dreaming.* Northvale, NJ/London: Jason Aronson.

Oliver, M. (1992). *New and Selected Poems.* Boston: Beacon Press.

Oremland, J. (1997). *The Origins and Psychodynamics of Creativity: A Psychoanalytic Perspective.* Madison, CT: International Universities Press.

Orwell, G. (1949/1981). Reflections on Gandhi. In *A Collection of Essays,* pp. 172–180. San Diego, New York, London: Harcourt, Brace.

Ozick, C. (1983). *Art and Ardor.* New York: Knopf.

Pascal, B. (1958). *Pensées.* New York: Dutton.

Phillips, A. (1988). *Winnicott.* Cambridge: Harvard University Press.

———. (1993) *On Kissing, Tickling, and Being Bored: Psychoanalytic Essays on the Unexamined Life.* Cambridge: Harvard University Press.

———. (1994). *On Flirtation: Psychoanalytic Essays on the Uncommitted Life.* Cambridge: Harvard University Press.

———. (1995). *Terrors and Experts.* Cambridge: Harvard University Press.

———. (1998). *The Beast in the Nursery.* New York: Pantheon Books.

Pirke Aboth: The Ethics of the Fathers. (1945). Trans. J. Tepfer. New York: Schocken.

Prilleltensky, I. (1997). Values, assumptions, and practices: Assessing the moral implications of psychological discourse and action. *American Psychologist,* 52(5): 517–535.

Rank, O. (1932). *Art and Artist: Creative Urge and Personality Development.* New York/London: W. W. Norton.

Ricoeur, P. (1970). *Freud and Philosophy: An Essay on Interpretation.* New Haven & London: Yale University Press.

Rieff, P. (1959). *Freud: The Mind of the Moralist.* New York: Harper & Row.

Roland, A. (1996). *Cultural Pluralism and Psychoanalysis: The Asian-American Experience.* New York: Routledge.

Rorty, R. (1986). Freud and Moral Reflection. In Joseph Smith & William Kerrigan (Eds.), *Pragmatism's Freud: The Moral Disposition of Psychoanalysis.* Baltimore: John Hopkins University Press, pp. 1–27.

Rosenau, P. (1993). *Post-Modernism and the Social Sciences.* Princeton: Princeton University Press.

Rothenberg, A. (1990). Psychotherapy and Creativity. In *Creativity and Madness: New Findings and Old Stereotypes*. Baltimore: John Hopkins University Press, pp. 165–180.

Rubin, J. B. (1996). *Psychotherapy and Buddhism: Toward and Integration*. New York: Plenum Press.

———. (1997). Psychoanalysis Is Self-Centered. In C. Spezzano & J. Garguilo (Eds.), *Soul on the Couch*. Hillsdale, NJ: Analytic Press.

———. (1997a). Reflections on values and morality in psychoanalysis. *Psychologist-Psychoanalyst*, 27(1): 17–20.

———. (1998). *A Psychoanalysis for Our Time: Exploring the Blindness of the Seeing I*. New York: New York University Press.

———. (1999). Religion, Freud, and women. *Gender and Psychoanalysis*, 4(4): 333–365.

———. (2001). Reflections on Values in Psychoanalysis. In A. Molino (Ed.), *Where Id Was: Normalization in Psychoanalysis*. London & New York: Continuum, pp. 217–221.

———. (2003). A Well-Lived Life: Psychoanalytic and Buddhist Contributions. In J. Safran (Ed.), *Psychoanalysis and Buddhism: An Unfolding Dialogue*. Boston: Wisdom Publications, pp. 387–425.

Rycroft, C. (1968). *Imagination and Reality*. London: Maresfield Library.

Safran, J. (Ed.) (2003). *Psychoanalysis and Buddhism: An Unfolding Dialogue*. Boston: Wisdom Publications.

Salman, S. (1997). The Creative Psyche: Jung's Major Contributions. In P. Young-Eisendrath & T. Dawson (Eds.), *The Cambridge Companion to Jung*. New York: Cambridge University Press, pp. 52–70.

Schafer, R. (1976). *A New Language for Psychoanalysis*. New Haven & London: Yale University Press.

Schuyler, J. (1993). Hymn to Life. In *Collected Poems*. New York: Farrar Straus & Giroux.

Segal, S. (Ed.) (2003). *Encountering Buddhism: Western Psychology and Buddhist Teachings*. Albany: State University of New York Press.

Sexton, A. (1981). *The Collected Poems*. Boston: Houghton Mifflin.

Shakespeare, W. (1964). *The Sonnets, Songs, and Poems of Shakespeare*. O. J. Campbell (Ed.). New York: Schocken Books.

Shinder, J. (Ed.) (2000). *Tales from the Couch: Writers on Therapy*. New York: William Morrow.

Smith, H. (1982). The Sacred Unconscious. In *Beyond the Postmodern Mind*. Wheaton, IL: Theosophical Publishing House, pp. 177–185.

Sorenson, R. (1994). On-going change in psychoanalytic theory: Implications for analysis of religious experience. *Psychoanalytic Dialogues*, 4: 631–660.

Spezzano, C., & Garguilo, J. (Eds.) (1997). *Soul on the Couch: Spirituality, Religion, and Morality in Psychoanalysis*. Hillsdale, NJ: Analytic Press.

Steiner, G. (1989). *Real Presences*. Chicago: University of Chicago Press.

Stoller, R. (1985). *Observing the Erotic Imagination*. New Haven: Yale University Press.

Stolorow, R., & Atwood, G. (1979). *Faces in a Cloud: Subjectivity in Personality Theory*. New York: Jason Aronson.

—————, Brandchaft, B., & Atwood, G. (1987). *Psychoanalytic Treatment: An Intersubjective Approach*. Hillsdale, NJ: Analytic Press.

Storr, A. (1988). Psychoanalysis and Creativity. In *Churchill's Dog, Kafka's Mice, and Other Phenomena of the Human Mind*. New York: Grove.

Strenger, C. (1997). Psychoanlysis as art and discipline of the self: A late modern perspective. *Psychoanalysis and Contemporary Thought*: 20(1): 69–110.

—————. (1997b). Further reflections on the classic & the romantic visions in psychoanalysis: Klein, Winnicott, and Ethics. *Psychoanalysis and Contemporary Thought*, 20(2): 207–243.

Suler, J. (1993). *Contemporary Psychoanalysis and Eastern Thought*. Albany: State University of New York Press.

Suttie, I. (1935). *The Origins of Love and Hate*. Harmondsworth, England: Penguin Books.

Suzuki, S. (1970). *Zen Mind, Beginner's Mind*. New York: Weatherhill.

Symington, N. (1994). *Emotion and Spirit: Questioning the Claims of Psychoanalysis and Religion*. New York: St. Martin's Press.

Taylor, C. (1989). *Sources of the Self: The Making of the Modern Identity*. Cambridge: Harvard University Press.

—————. (1991). *The Ethics of Authenticity*. Cambridge: Harvard University Press.

Todorov, T. (1996). Letter from Paris. *Salmagundi*, Winter-Spring (Number 109–110): 3–15.

—————. (1997). The labor of love. *Partisan Review*, 64(3): 375–383.

Tolstoy, L. *The Death of Ivan Ilyich*. Trans. Rosemary Edmonds. Harmondsworth, England: Penguin Books.

Ulanov, A. (1985). A Shared Space. *Quadrant*, 18(1): 65–80.

—————. (2001). *Finding Space: Winnicott, God, and Psychic Reality*. Louisville, KY: Westminster John Knox Press.

—————. & Ulanov, B. (1994). *Transforming Sexuality: The Archetypal World of Anima and Animus*. Boston & London: Shambhala.

Ullman, M., & Zimmerman, N. (1979). *Working with Dreams*. Los Angeles: Jeremy Tarcher.

—————. (1996). *Appreciating Dreams*. London: Sage.

—————, & Limmer, C. (1999). *The Variety of Dream Experience: Expanding Our Ways of Working with Dreams*. Albany: State University of New York Press.

Viederman, M. (1988). The Nature of Passionate Love. In W. Gaylin & E. Person (Eds.), *Passionate Attachments: Thinking about Love*. New York: Free Press, pp. 1–14.

Wallwork, E. (1988). A Constructive Freudian Alternative to Psychotherapeutic Egoism. In Charles Reynolds & Ralph Norman (Eds.), *Community in America: The Challenges of Habits of the Heart*. Los Angeles & Berkeley: University of California Press, pp. 202–214.

Walsh, R. (1981). Speedy Western Minds Slow Slowly. *Revision*, 4: 75–77.

Wilkinson, S. M., & Gabbard, G. (1995). On romantic space. *Psychoanalytic Psychology*, 12(2): 201–219.

Williams, R. (1989). *Resources of Hope*. London: Verso.

Winnicott, D. W. ([1951] 1978). Transitional Objects and Transitional Phenomena. In *Through Paediatrics to Psycho-Analysis*. London: Hogarth Press, pp. 229–242.

———. (1971). *Playing and Reality*. London: Tavistock Publications.

———. (1986). *Home Is Where We Start From: Essays by a Psychoanalyst*. Harmondsworth, England: Penguin Books.

Wittgenstein, L. (1953). *Philosophical Investigations*. New York: Macmillan.

———. (1980). *Culture and Value*. Chicago: University of Chicago Press.

Wolstein, B. (1993). Book Review in *Psychoanalytic Review*, 80, no. 4: 66.

Wordsworth, W. (1984). The Tables Turned: An Evening Scene, On the Same Subject. In *William Wordsworth: The Major Works*. Oxford: Oxford University Press, pp. 130–131.

Yalom, I. (1989). *Love's Executioner and Other Tales of Psychotherapy*. New York: Harper-Collins.

Yeats, W. B. (1971). Crazy Jane with the Bishop. In P. Allt & R. Alspach (Eds.), *The Variorum Edition of the Poems of W. B. Yeats*. New York: Macmillan.

Zuckerberg, J. (1985). Eros and classical considerations. *International Forum of Psychoanalysis*, 4: 231–237.

INDEX

123